Ancient Egypt for Beginners

The Story of the Land of the Pharaohs Simplified for People Who Slept Through History Class

Free Bonus from Captivating History
(Available for a Limited time)

Hi History Lovers!

Now you have a chance to join our exclusive history list so you can get your first history ebook for free as well as discounts and a potential to get more history books for free!

Simply visit the link below to join.

Or, Scan the QR code!

captivatinghistory.com/ebook

Also, make sure to follow us on Facebook, X, and YouTube by searching for Captivating History.

Table of Contents

Introduction:
Why Ancient Egypt Still Matters

Picture this: while some people's ancestors were huddling in caves and figuring out which berries wouldn't kill them, the ancient Egyptians were building structures so massive and precise that people today still argue about how they pulled it off. They invented a writing system that began with over seven hundred symbols and expanded to thousands over time. They practiced early forms of cranial surgery to treat head injuries. They created a civilization that lasted three thousand years—that's longer than the time between the fall of Rome and today.

To put that in perspective, Cleopatra lived over two thousand years after the Great Pyramid was built, making her temporally closer to us than to its construction. When travelers visited Egypt during the Roman Empire, the pyramids were already ancient monuments that the Romans had inscribed with their own graffiti.

So why does ancient Egypt still grab our attention? Why do museums pack exhibitions of Egyptian artifacts with crowds? Why does a boy king who died young and had a relatively unremarkable political career remain one of the most famous people in history?

It's because ancient Egypt had it all. It had drama worthy of any modern soap opera—family betrayals, religious revolutions, mysterious deaths. There were military campaigns and empire-building that would make any strategy game player jealous. And we can't forget the engineering feats that baffle experts, even with our modern technology.

Perhaps most fascinating of all, the ancient Egyptians' obsession with death and the afterlife produced some of the most elaborate burial practices humanity has ever devised.

But ancient Egypt wasn't just flash and spectacle. It was a functional, sophisticated society that fed millions of people, maintained law and order, conducted international diplomacy, and created art and literature that still move us today. They did all of this without computers, electricity, or any of the technology we consider essential. They had the Nile River, human ingenuity, and an impressive ability to organize large numbers of people toward common goals.

This book will take you through the entire sweep of ancient Egyptian civilization, from around 3100 BCE when the land was first unified under a single ruler all the way to 30 BCE when Cleopatra died and Egypt became a province of the Roman Empire. That's roughly three millennia of history—longer than most civilizations have existed.

You don't need any prior knowledge about Egypt or ancient history. This book assumes you're starting from scratch, maybe with a few images of pyramids in your head and a vague memory of hearing about King Tut. That's perfect. We'll build up your understanding piece by piece, explaining everything as we go. This won't be a long, boring list of ruler after ruler either. We want to make sure you leave this book with the understanding of how people lived back then and the most important figures who impacted the land.

So let's journey back three thousand years and discover the land of the pharaohs. Welcome to ancient Egypt.

Chapter 1: Before the Pharaohs— The Gift of the Nile

Geography Is Destiny

If you want to understand ancient Egypt, you need to understand one simple fact: the Nile River made everything possible.

Without the Nile, Egypt would be nothing but an empty desert stretching from the Mediterranean Sea to central Africa. With the Nile, Egypt became one of the most powerful civilizations in history. The river didn't just provide water. It also provided life itself, and it shaped every aspect of Egyptian culture, religion, economy, and politics for thousands of years.

The Nile is the longest river in Africa, flowing roughly 4,160 miles from its sources in the heart of the continent northward to the Mediterranean. However, ancient Egyptians only controlled and cared about the final stretch, roughly 750 miles of valleys and deltas.

Unlike most rivers that flood unpredictably and destructively, the Nile's annual inundation usually followed a reliable pattern, though occasionally the floods failed or came too strong. Every summer, heavy rains in the Ethiopian Highlands would swell the river. By late July or early August, the floodwaters would reach Egypt, slowly rising over the riverbanks and spreading across the floodplain. The water would sit there for months, depositing rich, dark silt—essentially free fertilizer—across the fields. Then, just as predictably, the waters would recede in October, leaving behind moist, nutrient-rich soil perfect for planting.

This gave the ancient Egyptians a tremendous advantage. While the Nile's silt provided rich baseline nutrients, Egyptian farmers supplemented the soil with manure and ashes, and they practiced basic field management. Still, they didn't need to pray for rain or worry about droughts the way farmers in Mesopotamia did. They just needed to wait for the Nile to do its thing and then plant their seeds in the fresh mud. The system was so reliable that Egyptians divided their entire calendar around it: Akhet (inundation), Peret (growing season), and Shemu (harvest).

The result was an abundance of crops that could support a large population without everyone needing to farm. That freed people up to become craftsmen, priests, soldiers, scribes, and builders. In other words, the Nile's predictable flooding made civilization possible.

But here's where geography gets confusing for modern readers: Upper Egypt is in the south, and Lower Egypt is in the north.

Yes, you read that correctly. Upper Egypt is downstream from Lower Egypt. This seems backward until you remember that ancient Egyptians were thinking about elevation and the river's flow, not compass directions. The Nile flows from south to north, from the highlands down to the sea. Upper Egypt, in the south, is upriver and at a higher elevation. Lower Egypt, in the north, is downriver and at a lower elevation where the river spreads into the delta before reaching the Mediterranean.

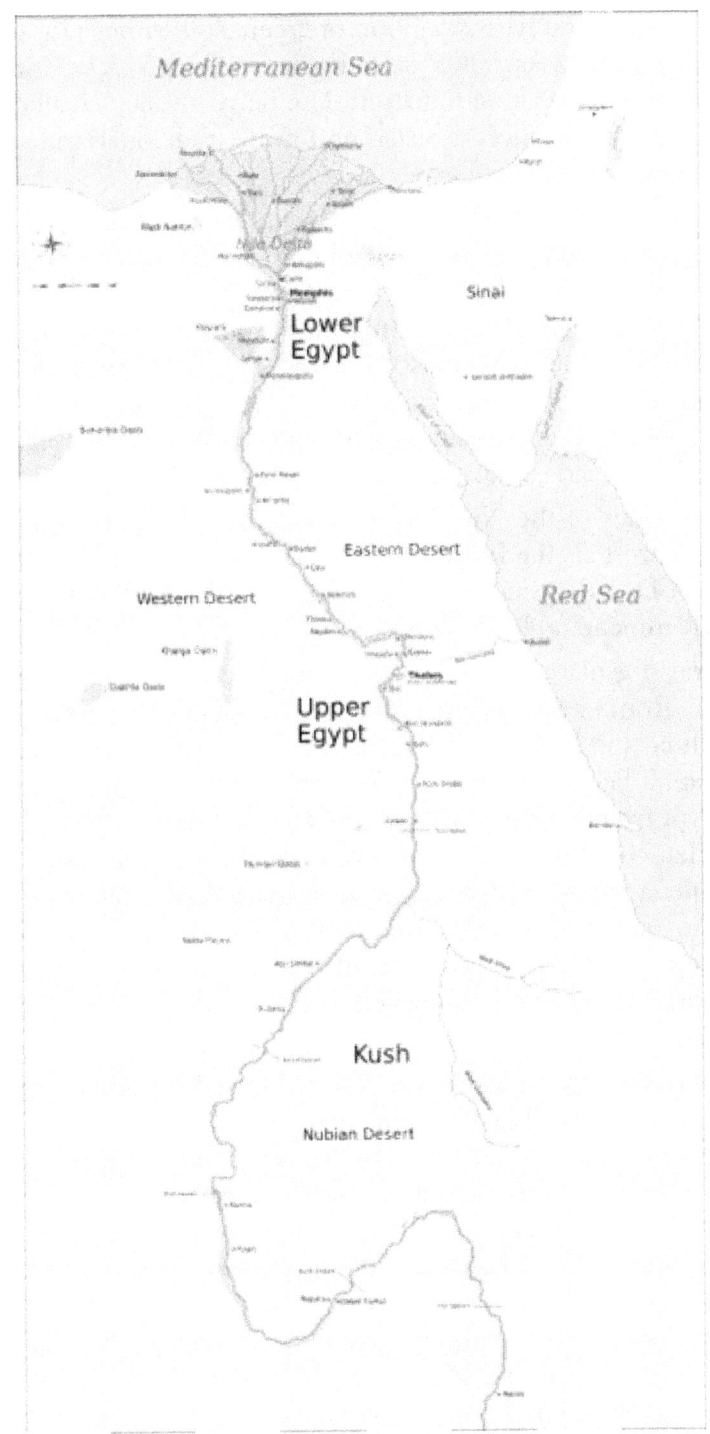

A map of Upper and Lower Egypt.[1]

Upper Egypt was a narrow ribbon of green, sometimes just a few miles wide, squeezed between cliffs and desert on both sides. Communities there were strung out along the river. The narrow valley created a certain kind of culture; it was more isolated and more traditional, with each town having a strong local identity.

Lower Egypt was completely different. Here, the Nile split into multiple branches and spread across a broad delta roughly 150 miles wide. The delta was a patchwork of marshes, channels, and fertile islands. It was lush, green, and soggy. This region could produce even more food than the narrow valley, but it was also more vulnerable to invasion from the Mediterranean or from neighboring regions in the Near East. The delta's culture reflected this openness. It was more cosmopolitan, more influenced by foreign contact, and more commercially minded.

On both sides of the Nile Valley stretched vast expanses of sand and rock. To the west lay the Libyan Desert, part of the Sahara. To the east lay the Arabian Desert, rising to mountains along the Red Sea coast. These were nearly impenetrable barriers.

This was Egypt's great advantage. The deserts provided significant protection from invasion that few other ancient cultures enjoyed. Mesopotamia, for instance, sat on a flat plain with no natural barriers, which meant it faced constant invasions and conquests. Any army trying to invade Egypt from the west or east would have to cross hundreds of miles of desert that could devastate an entire force through thirst and heat. The Mediterranean protected the north, and a series of cataracts (rapids) on the Nile made invasion from the south difficult. While these barriers weren't impenetrable—Egypt eventually faced successful invasions from the Levant, Nubia, and elsewhere—they made conquest far more challenging.

However, this protection came with increased isolation compared to other regions. While Egypt maintained important trade routes to the Levant, Nubia, Sinai, Punt, and across the Mediterranean, the desert barriers reduced casual contact with neighboring peoples. This geographical situation, combined with deliberate cultural policy, led to a kind of conservatism in Egyptian culture. Egyptians developed a certain worldview that their land was the center of creation, the only truly civilized place. They called their country "Kemet," meaning "the Black Land," referring to the rich, dark soil. Everything beyond the fertile strip was "Deshret," the "Red Land"—the lifeless desert.

Of course, the deserts provided some benefits beyond defense. They contained valuable resources, like gold mines, copper deposits, and various types of stone for building and sculpture. The eastern desert offered access routes to the Red Sea, enabling trade with Punt (likely modern Somalia or Eritrea) and other distant lands. The western desert had a string of oases that could support small populations and serve as waypoints for trade routes reaching into Africa.

Even so, over 95 percent of the ancient Egyptian population lived within a few miles of the Nile. Step away from the Nile in most places, and you'd be in a barren wasteland. This created a particular mindset. Egyptians saw their world as an island of order and abundance surrounded by chaos and death. The Nile was the source of life, the gift of the gods, and the reason Egypt existed at all. This reverence for the river would shape Egyptian religion, with the Nile itself deified and its annual flood celebrated as a divine blessing.

Geography also influenced Egyptians in ways that wouldn't become clear until later. The narrow river valley naturally connected communities. Boats could travel the entire length of Egypt, moving goods and people efficiently. The current flowed north, but the prevailing winds blew south, meaning one could sail upriver and float downriver. This made the Nile a natural highway. When Egypt eventually unified under a single ruler, the river would serve as the literal and metaphorical spine of the kingdom.

So, before there were pharaohs or pyramids, before there was any such thing as "Egypt," there was the Nile, flooding faithfully every year, creating a green corridor through the desert, and making life possible in one of the most inhospitable regions on Earth. Everything that followed stemmed from this one geographical fact.

From Hunters to Farmers

Ten thousand years ago, Egypt looked nothing like the Egypt of the pharaohs. There were no pyramids, no temples, and no cities. There wasn't even much of a desert yet.

After the Last Ice Age, North Africa experienced what scientists call the African Humid Period, roughly 9000 to 5500 BCE. During this time, the Sahara wasn't a desert but a savanna, with grasslands, lakes, and seasonal rivers. Early humans hunted wild cattle and gazelle across landscapes that would later become barren sand. They gathered wild plants, fished in lakes that no longer exist, and lived as mobile hunter-gatherers following seasonal resources.

Around 5500 BCE, the climate began to change. North Africa started drying out. The humid period ended, and the Sahara began its gradual transformation into the desert we know today. This process took thousands of years, but by around 3500 BCE, as the land became more arid, people and animals had been pushed toward the few remaining water sources. The most reliable water source in the entire region was the Nile.

This was the time when agriculture came to Egypt, though Egyptians didn't invent it. Farming was first developed in the Fertile Crescent, the region stretching from modern Iraq through Syria to Israel, around 10,000 BCE. The knowledge of growing crops gradually spread to Egypt over thousands of years. By around 5000 BCE, communities along the Nile were growing wheat and barley, raising cattle, sheep, and goats, and living in permanent villages.

This shift from hunting and gathering to farming—what historians call the Neolithic Revolution—changed everything. When people settle down and farm, they can support larger populations. They accumulate possessions and develop crafts and specializations. Social hierarchies emerge. In short, they start building civilizations.

The archaeological evidence for this period comes from sites scattered along the Nile Valley. At places like Merimde Beni Salama in the western delta and El-Omari near modern Cairo, archaeologists found the remains of early farming villages dating to between 5000 and 4000 BCE. These weren't sophisticated settlements. Their homes were simple oval huts, sometimes partially dug into the ground. People stored grain in baskets and pots. They buried their dead in simple graves, sometimes right within the village.

But even in these early communities, we see signs of what would become characteristic Egyptian practices. The dead were buried with grave goods, like pots, tools, and jewelry, suggesting beliefs about an afterlife in which the deceased would need these items. Bodies were typically placed on their sides in a flexed position, often facing west, toward the setting sun. These burial customs would evolve but never fundamentally change throughout Egyptian history.

By around 4000 BCE, Egypt entered what archaeologists call the Predynastic Period. This was when things started getting interesting. Communities were growing larger and more complex. Villages were turning into towns. Trade networks were expanding, and distinct regional cultures were emerging.

The most important of these cultures was the Naqada culture, named after the site where archaeologists first identified it. The Naqada culture developed in Upper Egypt and went through three main phases, which archaeologists creatively named Naqada I, II, and III (dating roughly 4000–3000 BCE).

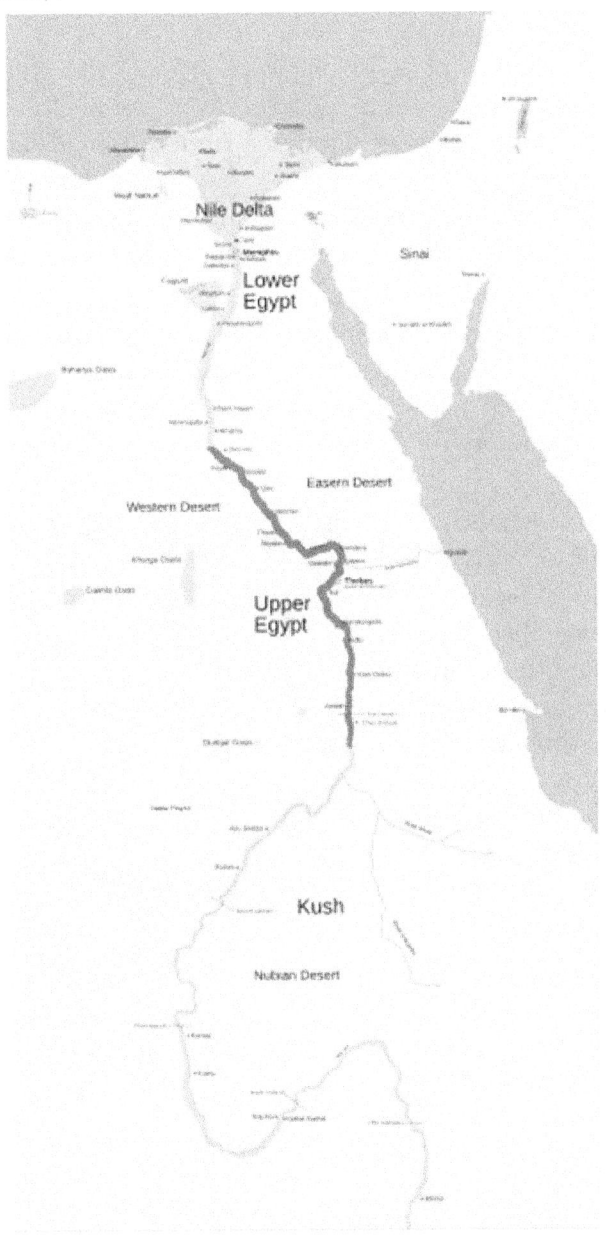

The extent of the Naqada culture.[3]

The Naqada I society was relatively simple. People lived in small agricultural communities, made distinctive pottery with geometric decorations, and created stone tools and weapons. However, there's evidence of growing social differentiation. Some burials are larger and contain more goods than others, suggesting that certain individuals had more wealth and status.

Naqada II marks the period of rapid change. Towns grew larger. Craft specialization increased—some people were now full-time potters, metalworkers, or stone carvers. Trade expanded dramatically, with goods moving long distances up and down the Nile. Egyptian-made objects started appearing in southern Palestine, and foreign goods showed up in Egypt. Copper became more common, and Egyptians were learning to work with it effectively.

The pottery from this period also changed dramatically. Instead of geometric patterns, Naqada II pottery featured painted scenes of boats, animals, humans, and mysterious symbols. Some of these images show boats carrying standards or banners that might represent early gods or tribal symbols.

Most importantly, the Naqada II society was clearly becoming hierarchical. Large tombs appeared that were far more elaborate than anything before. Some burials contained hundreds of pottery vessels, stone tools, jewelry, and other luxury goods. A few individuals were buried like chiefs or kings, suggesting that political leadership was becoming formalized.

During Naqada III (roughly 3200–3000 BCE), writing appeared in Egypt. There is debate over whether Egyptians invented writing independently or were inspired by early Mesopotamian writing systems— the concept of writing might have come from Mesopotamia,

A jar from the late Naqada II period.[*]

but the Egyptian system's form and symbols developed distinctly. The earliest Egyptian writing takes the form of simple labels and tags identifying the contents of storage jars or the ownership of goods. It was not literature yet—just basic record-keeping. But it was the beginning of the hieroglyphic system.

The archaeological record shows the emergence of powerful regional centers—basically proto-kingdoms—competing for control of the Nile Valley in the Naqada III period. Some towns were fortified with massive walls. Artistic depictions show warfare and conquest. Ceremonial objects show rulers smiting enemies and subduing towns.

One of these competing centers was Hierakonpolis (Egyptian name: Nekhen) in Upper Egypt. This was a major city for its time, with population estimates reaching as high as ten thousand people, though such figures are difficult to confirm. Excavations have revealed massive mudbrick walls, elite tombs, a temple complex, and a variety of ceremonial objects. Hierakonpolis was clearly one of the most powerful centers in late Predynastic Egypt.

Another important center was This (or Thinis), farther north in Upper Egypt. Less is known about This because the site hasn't been definitively located, but historical texts identify it as the home city of Egypt's first kings. It was probably the rival to Hierakonpolis for dominance in Upper Egypt.

Meanwhile, Lower Egypt had its own distinct culture and probably its own powerful chiefdoms, though we know less about them. The delta is harder for archaeologists to study because thousands of years of Nile flooding have buried or destroyed most early sites. However, texts and imagery from the Early Dynastic Period reference Lower Egyptian kingdoms that had to be conquered during Egypt's unification.

The archaeological evidence for this period is frustratingly incomplete, but what we have paints a picture of an increasingly sophisticated political organization. Large ceremonial buildings appear at sites like Hierakonpolis and Abydos. Massive tombs were constructed for elite individuals, some with multiple chambers and large quantities of luxury goods. We also start seeing standardized symbols, particularly the serekh, a rectangular frame topped with a falcon that represented royal authority. These weren't just decorative. They were political statements and markers of kingship.

The rulers of these early kingdoms weren't called pharaohs yet—that title came later. But they wielded real power. They commanded labor for building projects, controlled trade routes, and led military forces. Some of them were wealthy enough to be buried with hundreds of pottery vessels, stone tools, copper implements, and jewelry made from exotic materials like lapis lazuli from Afghanistan or obsidian from Ethiopia.

One site that gives us a particularly clear picture of this period is Cemetery U at Abydos in Upper Egypt. Here, archaeologists discovered a series of large tombs dating to around 3200 to 3100 BCE. The most impressive belonged to a ruler designated "Scorpion I" (named after the scorpion symbol found in his tomb). This wasn't a simple grave. It was a complex of multiple rooms covering over forty square meters, filled with hundreds of imported jars from southern Palestine that probably contained wine and other valuable liquids. The wine alone—expensive imported luxury goods—represented enormous wealth. The tomb also contained ivory artifacts, stone vessels, and remnants of what might have been an early form of hieroglyphic writing.

The existence of such elaborate tombs tells us several things. First, these rulers controlled enough resources and labor to construct substantial burial monuments. Second, they were engaged in long-distance trade networks stretching to Palestine and beyond. Third, they believed in an afterlife that would require furnishings and provisions—a belief that would become central to Egyptian culture. And fourth, they felt secure enough in their power to advertise it through conspicuous consumption and display.

But the most telling evidence comes from the imagery that appears on objects from this period. Carved stone palettes, ceremonial maceheads, and decorated pottery show scenes of warfare and domination, including bound captives and walled towns being attacked.

Two crowns became important symbols. The White Crown was associated with Upper Egypt—a tall, bowling-pin-shaped hat. The Red Crown represented Lower Egypt. It had a more complex design, with a tall back and a protruding spiral in front. Later, when Egypt was unified, pharaohs would wear both crowns, either separately or combined into the Double Crown, to emphasize their rule over both regions.

But in the late Predynastic Period, these crowns represented rival kingdoms. Upper Egypt, stretching from roughly modern Aswan to the area around Memphis, was probably the more unified and powerful region by 3200 BCE. Lower Egypt in the delta was likely divided among multiple competing centers, though evidence is limited due to poor preservation in the marshy delta. The historical tradition, recorded much later, claims that there were separate kings of Upper and Lower Egypt before unification, though we can't be certain of the details.

What's crucial to understand about the Predynastic Period is that Egypt wasn't marching inevitably toward unification. Multiple powerful centers were competing with each other. There were probably periods of warfare, alliances, trade relations, and cultural exchange. Different regions had somewhat different pottery styles, burial customs, and artistic traditions.

What we can say is that by around 3100 BCE, one of the Upper Egyptian kingdoms had emerged as dominant. This kingdom, based at either Hierakonpolis or This, had conquered or absorbed its neighbors and controlled the entire southern region. Its rulers had wealth, military power, and ambition. And they were looking north toward the delta.

Why did unification happen when it did? Several factors likely played a role.

Population growth and agricultural expansion might have created pressure for territorial control. More people meant more competition for prime farmland along the Nile. Kingdoms that could control longer stretches of the river had access to more resources and could support larger populations and armies.

Control of trade routes also mattered. The delta was the gateway to the Mediterranean and to trade with the Near East. Access to imported goods—cedar wood from Lebanon, silver from Anatolia, wine and oil from Palestine—was both economically valuable and politically significant, as luxury goods reinforced a ruler's status.

Military technology was improving as well. Copper weapons were becoming more common, giving armies that could afford to equip their soldiers with metal blades an advantage over those still using stone. Organizational sophistication was also increasing, as rulers could mobilize larger forces and sustain longer campaigns.

Another factor was that the concept of kingship was becoming more developed. Rulers claimed divine sanction, presenting themselves as necessary for maintaining cosmic order. A kingdom that could project this image of divinely sanctioned authority more effectively might find it easier to legitimize its expansion.

Finally, there was probably an element of historical accident and individual ambition. Unification required a ruler capable of imagining and executing a conquest of the entire Nile Valley. Not every generation produces such a person.

By 3200 BCE, Egypt was like a pot of water just about to boil. All the necessary ingredients for civilization were present: agricultural surplus, urban centers, social hierarchy, craft specialization, long-distance trade, writing, organized religion, and political leadership. By 3100 BCE, all the pieces were in place. Upper Egypt had a powerful king with military resources and territorial ambitions. Lower Egypt was probably divided and vulnerable. The technological, economic, and ideological tools for state-building had been developed. What happened next would transform this collection of competing chiefdoms into a unified kingdom.

But that unification wasn't inevitable, and it didn't happen peacefully. It would take conquest and a powerful king.

Chapter 2: The Birth of a Civilization—Unification and the Early Dynastic Period

Narmer/Menes: The First Pharaoh

Around 3100 BCE, something remarkable happened along the Nile. For the first time, the entire stretch of river from the Mediterranean delta to the First Cataract came under the control of a single ruler. Egypt became one kingdom, and the age of the pharaohs began. (An interesting side note: Early rulers of Egypt were not known as pharaohs. This term was later used by rulers in the New Kingdom. The label was retroactively applied to previous Egyptian kings.)

The man credited with this achievement is known by two names: Narmer and Menes. Egyptian tradition, recorded thousands of years later by the priest Manetho, identified Menes as the founder of the First Dynasty and the unifier of Egypt. However, the archaeological evidence points to a king named Narmer, whose name appears on monuments dating to this period. Many scholars today believe Narmer and Menes are the same person, though this remains debated. Some suggest Menes might have been Narmer's successor, Hor-Aha, or that "Menes" was a throne name, title, or even a purely symbolic figure representing the unification itself rather than a specific individual.

What we can say with confidence is that a powerful Upper Egyptian king unified Egypt around 3100 BCE. The most important evidence for this unification comes from one of ancient Egypt's most famous artifacts: the Narmer Palette.

The Narmer Palette is a ceremonial stone slab, just over two feet tall, carved from a single piece of siltstone. It was discovered at Hierakonpolis in 1898. Both sides are covered with carved relief scenes.

On one side, Narmer wears the White Crown of Upper Egypt. He's shown in the classic pose that would be repeated thousands of times throughout Egyptian history: the king, larger than anyone else, raises a mace to strike a kneeling enemy he grabs by the hair. Behind Narmer stands a servant carrying his sandals. Above the captive, a falcon (representing the god Horus) perches on papyrus plants (symbolizing Lower Egypt) and holds a rope attached to a man's head (a symbolic representation of Upper Egypt's conquest of the north). Below Narmer's feet, two more enemies lie defeated.

The other side shows Narmer wearing the Red Crown of Lower Egypt, suggesting he now rules both regions. He's shown in a procession with standard bearers, inspecting rows of decapitated enemies, their severed heads placed between their legs. These violent scenes likely represent ritual motifs and symbolic royal power—the king as a victorious warrior—rather than documenting historical events. At the bottom of this side, a bull (representing the king's strength) breaks through the walls of a fortified town.

The palette shows us propaganda, not a detailed historical account. So, how did this unification actually happen? The process probably involved both military conquest and political maneuvering. By 3100 BCE, Upper Egypt had already consolidated into a single powerful kingdom, probably centered at This or Hierakonpolis. Lower Egypt seems to have been divided among multiple competing centers, though poor archaeological preservation in the marshy delta makes this difficult to confirm definitively. An Upper Egyptian king with sufficient military force and organizational skill could conquer the delta piece by piece, absorbing or destroying rival kingdoms one at a time.

The conquest wasn't necessarily quick. Based on the scale of the task, it might have taken years or even decades. Some delta rulers might have submitted without major battles, accepting vassal status under the Upper Egyptian king. Others were probably conquered by force, which would explain the violent imagery on the Narmer Palette and other objects from this period.

Once conquered, Lower Egypt had to be held. This required establishing new administrative centers, installing loyal officials, and projecting royal power throughout the delta. It meant demonstrating that resistance was futile and submission was rewarded. It also required creating powerful symbols of unity that legitimized the new political order.

This was where the symbolism of the Two Lands became crucial. Egypt would forever after be defined as the union of Upper and Lower Egypt—two distinct regions brought together under one pharaoh. The king wore both crowns, carried both sets of royal regalia, and was called "Lord of the Two Lands." Even the hieroglyphic writing of the word "Egypt" showed this duality, depicting both the papyrus plant of the north and the sedge plant of the south bound together.

Memphis, situated at the junction where the Nile Valley meets the delta, became Egypt's administrative center. It was neutral ground in a sense; it was not the old capital of either Upper or Lower Egypt, but a new city positioned to control both regions. From Memphis, a pharaoh could send messages and officials north into the delta or south into the valley with equal ease. The city would remain one of Egypt's most important administrative centers throughout most of Egyptian history, though other cities like Thebes and Amarna would sometimes serve as capitals or royal residences.

The establishment of Memphis marked the beginning of what Egyptologists call the Early Dynastic Period (approximately 3100–2686 BCE), which encompasses the First and Second Dynasties. This was the formative period of Egyptian civilization.

The Early Dynastic Period (3100–2686 BCE)

The Early Dynastic Period saw the basic structures of Egyptian civilization take shape: the institutions of government, the ideology of kingship, the development of writing, the establishment of trade networks, and the creation of a distinctive Egyptian artistic style.

It's frustrating that we don't know as much about this period as we'd like. The Early Dynastic Period left fewer monuments and inscriptions than later eras. Many royal tombs were plundered in antiquity. The written sources from this time are limited, mostly consisting of labels, seal impressions, and short inscriptions rather than detailed historical texts. What we know comes primarily from archaeology, and archaeology can answer only so many questions.

The First Dynasty included around eight to ten kings, though the exact number and sequence are debated because some names appear in some king lists but not others. After Narmer/Menes came kings like Aha (whom some scholars identify as Menes), Djer, Djet, Den, and Qa'a. These names don't mean much to most people today, but these rulers transformed Egypt from a conquered territory into a functioning unified state.

What did these early pharaohs actually do? First off, they established the administration needed to run a unified kingdom. Egypt couldn't be governed by the pharaoh alone; it was too large. Running a unified kingdom stretching 750 miles required organization. The pharaoh couldn't personally oversee every field, every granary, and every workshop. He needed representatives throughout Egypt who could act with royal authority.

The most important official was the tjaty (often called "vizier" in English). He was essentially the prime minister. The vizier oversaw the administration, heard legal cases, managed the treasury, directed public works, and reported directly to the pharaoh. It was one of the most powerful positions in Egypt. Viziers came from the highest ranks of the nobility.

Below the vizier were numerous specialized officials: regional governors controlling Egypt's provinces (nomes), overseers managing royal estates and workshops, treasurers tracking resources, scribes recording everything, military commanders, and high priests managing major temples. Officials were needed to collect taxes, record grain supplies, organize labor, manage irrigation systems, oversee trade, and enforce royal authority. The First Dynasty saw the development of this bureaucracy. Some positions were hereditary, passed from father to son, creating powerful families with generations of administrative experience. Others were appointed based on merit or royal favor.

Ancient Egyptians also developed writing during this period. The early hieroglyphic script that appeared at the end of the Predynastic Period was refined and expanded during the Early Dynastic Period. Writing was initially used for administrative purposes, but it was also used to record royal names and titles, helping to project royal authority and preserve their deeds.

The hieroglyphic writing system became increasingly sophisticated during this period. It used hundreds of signs. Some hieroglyphs were phonetic (representing sounds), some were logograms (representing whole words), and some were determinatives (indicating what category something belonged to). This made the system flexible but complex. It required years of training to master.

Alongside hieroglyphics, Egyptians began developing hieratic script, a more cursive form of writing better suited to being written quickly with a reed pen on papyrus. The earliest examples of hieratic appear late in the Early Dynastic Period. Hieratic would eventually be used for everyday administrative documents, while hieroglyphics remained reserved for formal inscriptions on stone monuments.

The administration ran on documentation. Scribes recorded crop yields, tax receipts, labor assignments, grain storage, and countless other details. This wasn't just bureaucratic fussiness; it was essential for managing resources in a pre-industrial economy. The government needed to know how much grain was in storage to survive low flood years, how much labor was available for construction projects, and how much revenue each province generated. Writing made this possible.

The economy was not monetary. Egypt wouldn't use coinage until the Late Period. Instead, transactions used barter, with values calculated in standard units like the deben (about 91 grams of copper). Workers were generally paid in rations—bread, beer, grain, and oil—though wages varied significantly by class and era. Taxes were collected in kind, which means farmers paid a portion of their harvest, and craftsmen paid in goods they produced. The government redistributed these resources to feed officials, priests, soldiers, and workers on royal projects.

The early pharaohs also developed royal ideology. The king wasn't just a powerful man. He was increasingly understood as divine, the living embodiment of the god Horus. Let's start with ma'at because nothing is more central to understanding how ancient Egyptians saw their world and why the pharaoh was so essential.

Ma'at is difficult to translate into English. It means truth, justice, order, balance, and harmony. It means the proper way things should be. Ma'at was simultaneously a concept, a goddess, and the fundamental principle underlying reality itself. While the principle of ma'at existed since the Early Dynastic Period, the philosophical articulations of the concept would come later, primarily in the Middle Kingdom.

In the Egyptian worldview, the universe existed in a delicate balance between ma'at (order) and isfet (chaos). Before creation, only isfet existed—a formless, chaotic, dark void. The creator god brought forth the ordered world from this chaos, establishing ma'at. But isfet didn't disappear. It constantly threatened to overwhelm creation and return everything to primordial chaos. Ma'at had to be actively maintained through proper behavior, ritual observance, and—most importantly—the actions of the pharaoh.

The king maintained ma'at through his very existence and through his actions. He was the legitimate ruler who maintained the cosmic order and stood between civilization and chaos. When the pharaoh ruled justly, performed the proper rituals, built temples for the gods, and defended Egypt's borders, he was literally holding the universe together. A weak or absent king didn't just create political problems; he also threatened cosmic disaster.

This concept had practical implications. It meant that proper order required a hierarchy. Everyone had their place, from the pharaoh at the top to farmers at the bottom. Social mobility existed, but it was limited. It meant that tradition and precedent were valued over innovation. Egyptians saw their civilization as special, as the one place where ma'at truly prevailed.

Ma'at also had ethical dimensions. Truth-telling, honesty, fairness in judgment, and proper treatment of subordinates weren't just nice ideas but also essential components of maintaining cosmic order. Officials were expected to uphold ma'at in their judgments. The dead would be judged based on whether they had lived according to ma'at. The concept provided something approaching a moral code, though one embedded in ideas about cosmic order rather than ethics.

Now, about the pharaoh himself. What did it mean to be a pharaoh in the Early Dynastic Period?

As we have established, the pharaoh was divine. He wasn't just a ruler chosen by gods; he was a god in human form. Specifically, he was the living Horus, the falcon god who was the legitimate king of Egypt. When a pharaoh died, he became identified with Osiris, the god of the dead, and his successor became the new Horus.

Royal names and titles became increasingly elaborate, emphasizing the king's divine nature and his role as intermediary between gods and humans. The pharaoh's title would eventually expand to five names. The most important was the Horus name, showing the king as the earthly manifestation of Horus. Later came the Two Ladies name (representing the protective goddesses of Upper and Lower Egypt), the Golden Horus name, the prenomen (throne name introduced by the phrase "King of Upper and Lower Egypt"), and the nomen (birth name introduced by "Son of Re").

Only a pharaoh and high-ranking priests could enter the innermost sanctuaries of temples where divine statues resided. The pharaoh performed rituals that ensured the gods' favor, the Nile's flooding, and the sun's daily journey across the sky. In temple reliefs, the pharaoh is always shown making offerings to the gods. In reality, priests performed most daily rituals, but they did so as the king's representatives, acting in his name.

The pharaoh owned all the land in Egypt. All officials served at his pleasure, and all resources were his to command. Any major decision required his approval or was made in his name. This doesn't mean a pharaoh micromanaged everything—the kingdom was too large for that—but theoretically, all power flowed from the king.

The pharaoh's image was carefully controlled. Royal statues and reliefs didn't show the king as he actually looked. They showed an idealized version emphasizing eternal, divine qualities. The pharaoh was always depicted as young and vigorous, with perfect proportions, a serene expression, and a commanding presence. This wasn't personal vanity; it was a theological necessity. The image had to reflect the king's divine nature and eternal role, not his mortal appearance.

This didn't mean pharaohs were puppet figures existing purely for ritual. Many were active rulers who made important decisions, led armies, directed building projects, and shaped policy. However, they operated within an ideological framework that defined them as divine beings maintaining cosmic order.

The early pharaohs built a lot of structures. The royal tombs at Abydos and Saqqara show increasingly sophisticated architecture. These weren't pyramids yet; that came later. Early royal tombs were elaborate mudbrick structures called mastabas (Arabic for "bench," describing their shape). These rectangular structures had underground burial chambers and above-ground chapels where offerings could be presented to the deceased king.

Some of these tombs were enormous. The tomb of King Den at Abydos featured a burial chamber accessed by a stone staircase—the first use of a staircase in Egyptian architecture. The tomb of Qa'a, the last king of the First Dynasty, had over thirty subsidiary chambers surrounding the main burial chamber, possibly used for storing grave goods.

But here's something disturbing about these early tombs: they were surrounded by subsidiary burials—graves of servants and officials buried at the same time as the king. It is widely believed that these individuals died when the king died. Either they were killed as part of the burial ritual, or they committed suicide to serve the king in the afterlife, though some scholars argue that some attendants might have been buried later or symbolically. This practice, called retainer sacrifice, appears in the First Dynasty but seems to have been abandoned by the Second Dynasty, possibly indicating changing religious beliefs or evolving attitudes about the afterlife.

Egypt had to expand its trade networks to support the state. Egyptian objects have been found in Palestine and Lebanon, while imported goods, like cedar wood, wine, and oil, appear in Egypt. Trade expeditions reached the Sinai Peninsula for copper and turquoise. Ships traveled to Byblos on the Lebanese coast to acquire cedar, which Egypt lacked but needed for large construction projects. Trade routes also extended south into Nubia for ivory, ebony, and gold. While some of these connections predated the dynasties, they developed significantly during the Early Dynastic Period.

The early pharaohs also conducted military campaigns. Egypt wasn't just consolidating internally; it was also projecting power beyond its borders. Rock inscriptions in Nubia suggest Egyptian military expeditions extended southward. The Sinai Peninsula, a source of copper and turquoise, came under Egyptian control. These campaigns secured resources, eliminated threats, demonstrated royal power, and provided opportunities for kings to fulfill their ideological role as mighty warriors who defended Egypt and expanded its borders.

The transition from the First to Second Dynasty around 2890 BCE seems to have involved some kind of political crisis, though the details are murky. The last king of the First Dynasty, Qa'a, was followed by kings who might have come from a different family line. There are hints in the archaeological record of instability. Some royal names were later erased, suggesting political conflict or a regime change.

The Second Dynasty continued the trends of the First Dynasty but seems to have been more troubled. Several kings left few traces, suggesting short or unsuccessful reigns. One king, Peribsen, did something unprecedented. Instead of using Horus as his patron deity, he chose Seth, Horus's rival in Egyptian mythology. Later, King Khasekhemwy used both Horus and Seth in his royal name, possibly indicating a reconciliation between competing factions that had divided Egypt.

The fact that Khasekhemwy's name means "The Two Powerful Ones Appear" suggests he was reunifying a divided Egypt. Whatever conflicts occurred during the Second Dynasty—and we can only guess at the details—they seem to have been resolved by the dynasty's end, setting the stage for the Old Kingdom and the age of pyramid building.

By the end of the Early Dynastic Period around 2686 BCE, Egypt had been transformed. The administrative apparatus could manage the kingdom's resources and mobilize large labor forces. Writing was used throughout the government. Trade networks extended throughout the eastern Mediterranean and into Africa. Royal ideology had developed to the point where the pharaoh was understood as a living god, the essential link between the divine and human realms. And Egyptian art had developed its distinctive style, focused on eternal order rather than fleeting moments.

All the pieces were in place. Egypt was ready for its first golden age, the Old Kingdom, when royal power and resources would be concentrated on the most ambitious building projects in human history: the pyramids.

Chapter 3: The Old Kingdom— When Egypt Built for Forever

Around 2686 BCE, Egypt entered what historians call the Old Kingdom, also known as the Pyramid Age. The Old Kingdom encompasses the Third Dynasty to the Sixth Dynasty. By the start of the Third Dynasty, Egypt had been unified for over four hundred years. The administrative systems were functioning smoothly. The ideology of divine kingship was firmly established. The economy was productive. Egypt was ready for something spectacular—monumental building on an unprecedented scale.

That something arrived in the form of King Djoser, the second ruler of the Third Dynasty, who reigned approximately 2667 to 2648 BCE. Djoser was probably a capable king who consolidated royal power and conducted military campaigns in the Sinai, but he would be remembered for building the world's first large-scale stone structure.

Before Djoser, Egyptian monuments were built from mudbrick and wood. These materials were practical. Mud from the Nile was abundant and easy to work with, and mudbrick structures could be quite impressive. But mudbrick crumbled over time. It couldn't achieve the heights or the permanence that stone offered. Stone had been used for certain elements, like doorframes and paving stones, but never for an entire monumental structure in Egypt on this scale.

Djoser's architect, a man named Imhotep, changed that. Imhotep is one of the most remarkable figures in ancient Egyptian history, and he is one of the few non-royal individuals to be remembered thousands of years later. He served as Djoser's chancellor and high priest, but his fame rests on his architectural achievement. Later Egyptian tradition revered Imhotep so much that he was eventually deified, worshiped as a god of wisdom and medicine. The Greeks would identify him with their god of healing, Asclepius. Two thousand years after his death, Egyptians still made pilgrimages to his supposed burial place.

What did Imhotep create that earned such lasting fame? He designed the Step Pyramid at Saqqara, just outside Memphis.

The Step Pyramid began as a traditional mastaba tomb, a rectangular mudbrick structure. However, Imhotep had a different vision. He expanded the mastaba, making it larger. Then he built another, smaller mastaba on top of it. Then another. And another. Eventually, he created a structure rising in six massive steps to a height of about 204 feet. It was the world's first pyramid, even if it didn't have the smooth sides we associate with later pyramids.

Djoser's Step Pyramid.*

The revolutionary aspect wasn't just the stepped design; it was also the material. Imhotep built in stone, specifically limestone quarried nearby and brought to the site. The Step Pyramid used an estimated 330,000 cubic meters of stone and clay—a monumental achievement.

The pyramid sat within a vast complex covering thirty-seven acres, surrounded by a limestone wall over thirty feet high. The complex included courtyards, chapels, ceremonial buildings, and storage rooms. Many of these structures served ritual purposes related to the king's afterlife or to ceremonies associated with royal power.

The Step Pyramid wasn't perfect. Some of the techniques were experimental, and parts of the structure were unstable. Some sections actually collapsed during construction and had to be rebuilt with buttressing walls. But as a first attempt at monumental stone architecture, it was astonishing.

Other Third Dynasty pharaohs attempted their own pyramids, with varying success. Sekhemkhet started a step pyramid but died before completing it. Khaba might have begun another. These projects show that kings learned from Djoser's example, though none matched his achievement during the Third Dynasty.

But these were just the beginning. The next dynasty would take Imhotep's innovation and perfect it, creating structures so iconic that they have become symbols of ancient Egypt itself. The Fourth Dynasty was approaching, and with it, the true Pyramid Age would arrive.

The Great Pyramids of Giza

The Fourth Dynasty (approximately 2613–2494 BCE) was ancient Egypt's architectural apex. Three kings of this dynasty—Khufu, Khafre, and Menkaure—built the pyramids at Giza that still dominate the landscape today. These structures are so massive and precise that they've become among the most recognizable monuments in the world.

The Fourth Dynasty didn't start at Giza. The dynasty's founder, Sneferu (approximately 2613–2589 BCE), was a prodigious builder who experimented with pyramid design and, in the process, built more total stone volume than any other pharaoh. Sneferu constructed at least three pyramids: the Pyramid at Meidum, the Bent Pyramid at Dahshur, and the Red Pyramid at Dahshur.

The Bent Pyramid is particularly significant because it shows Egyptian architects learning in real time. The pyramid starts at a steep angle—about fifty-four degrees—but about halfway up, the angle suddenly changes to a gentler forty-three degrees, creating the distinctive "bent" appearance. Why? Most likely, the steep angle created structural problems, and the architects decided mid-construction to reduce the angle to prevent collapse. The Bent Pyramid marks the transition from step pyramids to true smooth-sided pyramids.

The Bent Pyramid.[5]

Sneferu's Red Pyramid, built after the Bent Pyramid, achieved what earlier attempts had struggled to do: a true pyramid with smooth sides at a consistent angle from base to peak. At about 341 feet high, it was the world's tallest structure when completed. Sneferu had finally perfected the form.

The Red Pyramid.[6]

His son Khufu took this perfection and scaled it up dramatically. Khufu's Great Pyramid at Giza, built around 2560 BCE, is a structure almost beyond comprehension. Originally standing approximately 481 feet tall (now about 455 feet due to loss of the outer casing), it remained the world's tallest human-made structure for almost four thousand years. Its base covers approximately thirteen acres. It contains an estimated 2.3 million stone blocks, each weighing an average of 2.5 tons, though some blocks in the King's Chamber weigh up to 80 tons.

The precision is staggering. The base is level to within approximately 2.1 centimeters across its entire expanse. The sides are aligned almost perfectly to the cardinal directions with an error of only about 3.4 arc minutes (an arc minute is 1/60 of a degree). The blocks fit together so well that you often can't slip a knife blade between them. All of this was accomplished without iron tools (Egypt was still in the Copper Age), without the wheel for transportation, and without pulleys or cranes as we understand them.

So, how was it built? This question has fascinated people for millennia and has generated countless theories, from the plausible to the absurd. Let's focus on what archaeologists and engineers actually know.

The Greek historian Herodotus, who wrote 2,000 years after the pyramid's construction, claimed 100,000 slaves built it over 20 years. This is almost certainly wrong on both counts. According to recent archaeological evidence found in workers' villages and cemeteries, a permanent workforce of around five thousand skilled workers—quarrymen, masons, surveyors, and engineers—was supplemented during the annual flood season (when farm work was impossible) by a rotating labor force of perhaps twenty thousand to thirty thousand workers who hauled blocks and built ramps.

These weren't slaves in the sense Herodotus imagined. Archaeological evidence from workers' villages near the pyramids shows laborers were paid in food rations, received medical care, and had access to meat, which was a luxury for common Egyptians. Graffiti on blocks names work crews with designations like "Friends of Khufu" or "Drunkards of Menkaure," suggesting team pride rather than misery. The workers were organized into rotating crews from different regions, serving what was essentially a labor tax obligation.

Most of the limestone came from quarries near the pyramid site. Workers used copper tools and wooden wedges to split stone along natural bedding planes in the rock. Current evidence suggests blocks were then transported on wooden sledges pulled by teams of workers. Research and experimental archaeology show that wetting the sand ahead of sledges can reduce friction by up to 50 percent—a technique also depicted in Egyptian tomb paintings.

The granite blocks used for internal chambers came from Aswan, nearly six hundred miles south. These were transported by boat during the flood season when the Nile was high enough to bring the boats close to the pyramid site.

The lifting of the stones remains the most debated aspect. The most widely accepted theory involves ramps—probably a combination of a long external ramp for most of the construction and internal ramps or a spiral ramp for the upper levels. As the pyramid grew, the ramp was extended and raised. The ramp would have required almost as much material as the pyramid, but it could be dismantled, and the material could be reused afterward. Alternative theories have been proposed, including levers and cranes, but ramps remain the most practical explanation.

Building the Great Pyramid required extraordinary logistics. Stone had to be quarried, moved, and set in place at a rate of about one block every two minutes if the project took twenty years. This required precise planning, rotating work crews, a constant supply of food and water, tool maintenance, and oversight at every level. The project was likely divided into smaller units with a hierarchy of overseers coordinating everything.

The pyramid wasn't just the triangular structure we see today. It was part of a larger complex, including a mortuary temple where offerings were made to the deceased king, a causeway leading down to a valley temple at the Nile's edge, and smaller pyramids for queens. The entire complex served both the king's burial and his ongoing cult after death.

Khufu's son Khafre built the second pyramid at Giza. It was slightly smaller than his father's, but it appears to be taller because it was built on higher ground. Khafre also built, or at least completed, the Great Sphinx— that enormous limestone statue with a lion's body and a human head, probably representing the king himself. At 240 feet long and 66 feet high, the Sphinx is the world's largest monolithic statue carved from a single piece of bedrock.

Menkaure, Khafre's successor, built the third and smallest of the Giza pyramids, standing about 215 feet tall. While significantly smaller than his predecessors', it's still an enormous structure and features extensive use of granite from Aswan in its lower courses.

The Giza pyramids represent the peak of ancient Egyptian pyramid construction in terms of size and precision. Later pyramids would be built, but none would match these for sheer scale and accuracy. After the Fourth Dynasty, pyramid building continued, but with smaller structures and often shoddier construction.

The pyramids of Giza.'

Why did the Fourth Dynasty kings build on such a scale? These pharaohs had enormous resources at their disposal—a wealthy kingdom, productive agriculture, control of trade routes, and an effective administration. They believed profoundly in the afterlife and saw the pyramid as essential for their eternal existence. The pyramid was the pharaoh's stairway to the heavens, his permanent connection between earth and sky. Building such structures also demonstrated royal power, both to subjects and to the gods. A pharaoh who could move millions of tons of stone was clearly capable of maintaining ma'at and defending Egypt.

However, there may have been another factor: prestige and competition. Each king wanted to match or exceed his predecessors. Khufu built bigger than Sneferu. Khafre matched Khufu. This created an escalating cycle of monumental construction that consumed enormous resources, drove architectural innovation, and demonstrated Egypt's capabilities.

The pyramids have endured for over 4,500 years, weathering sandstorms, earthquakes, and attempts at dismantling (many later builders used pyramids as convenient quarries for pre-cut stone). They have inspired awe, wonder, and wild speculation. And they stand as testaments to what humans can achieve when vision, resources, organization, and determination align—even with Stone Age technology.

Life in the Pyramid Age

The pyramids dominate our view of the Old Kingdom, but they were built by a society, not by pharaohs alone. What was life actually like in Egypt during the Pyramid Age? How did ordinary people live while their kings built monuments that would last for eternity?

The Old Kingdom was a time of prosperity and stability for Egypt. The Nile flooded reliably, harvests were good, and the kingdom's borders were secure.

Egyptian society was hierarchical, organized in a clear pyramid itself. At the very top stood the pharaoh, the living god who, in theory, owned all of Egypt. Below him came the royal family and highest officials, such as viziers, high priests, and regional governors who wielded power and lived in luxury.

The next tier consisted of the professional classes: scribes, mid-level priests, skilled craftsmen, merchants, and military officers. These people lived comfortably, though not luxuriously. They had secure positions, steady food supplies, and the respect that came with specialized knowledge or skills.

Below them came the largest group: farmers, laborers, and unskilled workers. These people worked hard, often doing physical labor in harsh conditions, but they weren't slaves in the sense of being property. They had legal rights, could own property, and could seek justice in courts. Their lives were constrained by their position in the social hierarchy, but they were recognized as people with certain protections.

At the bottom of free society came various categories of dependent workers and servants, whose status was somewhere between free and enslaved. Slavery did exist in the Old Kingdom. They could be prisoners of war, criminals, or people who had fallen into debt slavery, though the scale of slavery was smaller than in some later periods or other ancient civilizations. However, it is important to emphasize that the massive building projects weren't built by slave labor; they were built by free workers fulfilling labor obligations to the state, a form of taxation paid in work rather than goods.

Social mobility was limited but not impossible. A talented scribe could rise to become a high official. A skilled craftsman might become overseer of a royal workshop. Merit could sometimes overcome birth, especially in the growing bureaucracy, which needed capable administrators.

Daily life for most Egyptians revolved around agriculture. The Nile's annual cycle dictated everything. During the inundation season (Akhet), when fields were flooded, farmers might be called up for state projects, like pyramid building. During the growing season (Peret), they planted and tended crops. They primarily grew wheat and barley, but they also raised flax for linen, vegetables, and fruits. During the harvest season (Shemu), they worked to bring in the crops before the next flood.

A typical farmer's day began at dawn. He'd eat a breakfast of bread and beer (both staples of the Egyptian diet) and then head to the fields with basic tools—hoes, sickles, and plows pulled by cattle. He'd work through the hot day, returning home at sunset to a simple house made of mudbrick.

Houses varied by social class. A wealthy official might have a large house with multiple rooms, a central courtyard, and even a garden with a pool. The walls would be plastered and painted. Furniture might include chairs, beds, and storage chests. A farmer's house might have just one or two rooms, minimal furniture (perhaps a sleeping platform and some baskets for storage), and a roof used for sleeping during hot nights.

The Egyptian diet was based on bread and beer. Bread wasn't like modern bread. It was coarse and often gritty with sand from the grinding stones, which explains why ancient Egyptian teeth show severe wear. Beer was thick, nutritious, and drunk by everyone, including children (it was safer than water). Those who could afford it supplemented this basic diet with vegetables (onions, garlic, lettuce, and cucumbers), fruits (dates, figs, and grapes), fish from the Nile, and occasionally meat (beef, pork, poultry, or wild game).

The wealthy ate much better, with more meat, elaborate preparations, honey for sweetening, and imported delicacies. Banquets depicted in tomb paintings show elaborate spreads with dozens of dishes, though these scenes likely represent idealized versions of the afterlife rather than everyday meals.

Clothing was simple. Men typically wore kilt-like garments made from linen, sometimes just a loincloth for laborers. Women wore straight linen dresses. The wealthy had finer linen, sometimes semi-transparent, and might wear jewelry made of gold, semi-precious stones, or faience beads. Children often went naked until puberty. Everyone went barefoot most of the time, though sandals made from papyrus or leather were worn when needed.

Family life was central. Marriages were arranged, but they seem to have generally been affectionate partnerships. Marriage required no official ceremony. A couple simply started living together, often with an agreement about property. Women had significant rights for the ancient world. They could own property, conduct business, initiate divorce, and inherit equally with men. A woman's primary role was managing the household and raising children, but she wasn't legally subordinate to her husband in the way women were in many ancient societies.

Children were valued and desired. Infant mortality was high, so families had multiple children, hoping several would survive to adulthood. Children helped with work from an early age, tending animals, helping in fields, or learning trades. Most children didn't receive a formal education, but boys from elite families would be sent to scribal schools around age nine to learn reading, writing, mathematics, and proper behavior. These schools were demanding, and corporal punishment was used freely. A saying from the time claims, "A boy's ear is on his back; he listens when he is beaten."

Recreation existed even in this work-focused society. Tomb paintings show people playing board games like senet and mehen, wrestling, dancing, and watching or participating in athletic competitions. Children played with toys, like dolls, balls, spinning tops, and toy animals. The wealthy enjoyed hunting in the desert or fowling in the marshes. Music was popular, featuring instruments such as harps, lutes, flutes, and drums.

Religion was a part of daily life. Egyptians believed in dozens of gods, each with specific domains and powers. Most people never entered the inner sanctuaries—those were for priests and the pharaoh—but they could pray at temple entrances, participate in festival processions, and worship at local shrines. Household worship was common, with small altars or shrines dedicated to protective deities.

Medical care existed, though it was limited by the era's understanding. Egyptian physicians could set broken bones, stitch wounds, and prescribe medicines made from plants, minerals, and animal products. Medical texts show they recognized different diseases and had specific treatments, though many remedies were more magical than practical. Still, Egyptian medicine was sophisticated for its time, and Egyptian doctors were renowned throughout the ancient world.

Trade connected Egypt to the wider world. Egyptian grain, linen, and papyrus were exported throughout the eastern Mediterranean. In return came cedar wood from Lebanon, olive oil and wine from the Levant, copper from Cyprus and Sinai, and luxury goods from farther afield, including lapis lazuli from Afghanistan, obsidian from Ethiopia, and ivory from Africa. This trade enriched the kingdom and exposed Egyptians to foreign ideas and goods.

The Old Kingdom was also a period of cultural flowering. This era produced some of ancient Egypt's finest art. Statues achieved remarkable naturalism within the conventions of the Egyptian style, reliefs were carved with exquisite detail, and tomb paintings depicted vivid scenes of daily life. The Pyramid Texts, the oldest known religious texts from ancient Egypt, were first inscribed on pyramid walls during the late Old Kingdom, preserving spells and sayings meant to guide the deceased king through the afterlife.

Literature began to develop, though most Old Kingdom texts were practical—administrative records, letters, or instructions. The great literary works would come later, but the foundations were being laid.

For most Egyptians, particularly those in the elite and professional classes, the Old Kingdom was likely a relatively good time to be alive compared to what came before or what they might have experienced in other ancient societies. The kingdom was stable during its peak, harvests were generally good in successful years, and the social order seemed secure. For farmers and laborers, life remained hard with the constant pressure of fulfilling obligations to landlords and the state, and local famines could still occur during poor flood years. If you were born a farmer, you'd die a farmer, but you'd live under a system that, for all its inequalities, provided order, justice (at least in theory), and the assurance that ma'at prevailed in Egypt while chaos ruled beyond the borders.

The pyramids rising on the western horizon weren't just monuments to dead kings. They were visible proof that Egypt was special, that the pharaoh maintained the cosmic order, and that the kingdom had the strength and organization to achieve the impossible. For the people who built them, hauling stones under the desert sun, the pyramids represented more than just a job. They were participating in something eternal, ensuring their king's successful journey to the afterlife, and contributing to Egypt's glory.

The Old Kingdom wouldn't last forever. By the late Sixth Dynasty, cracks were appearing in the seemingly eternal order. But at the time, Egypt was strong, prosperous, and confident. The pyramids would stand forever, and surely, the kingdom would too.

Chapter 4: Collapse and Chaos— The First Intermediate Period

When Central Power Failed

The Old Kingdom didn't end with a bang. There was no major foreign invasion, no dramatic rebellion that toppled the state, no sudden catastrophe. Instead, Egypt's first golden age faded gradually. One day, people looked around and realized the world had changed. The powerful centralized state that had built the pyramids was gone, replaced by fragmented regional powers and weakened kings. Egypt had entered what historians call the First Intermediate Period (approximately 2181-2055 BCE).

The collapse began during the Sixth Dynasty, which had started strongly but grew progressively weaker. The reign of Pepi II, who came to the throne as a child and ruled for an extraordinarily long time—possibly over sixty years, making him one of the longest-reigning monarchs in history—saw royal authority steadily erode. By the time Pepi II died, probably in his nineties, the centralized system his ancestors had built was crumbling.

What went wrong? Why did the seemingly eternal Old Kingdom fall apart?

The answer involves multiple factors, and historians debate which were most important. But several key problems converged to undermine the unified state.

First, there was an environmental crisis. Evidence from multiple sources, including Nile flood records, archaeological data, and climate studies, suggests that Egypt experienced a period of low Nile floods during the late Old Kingdom and early First Intermediate Period. When the Nile didn't flood properly, crops failed. When crops failed, people went hungry. When people went hungry, they couldn't pay taxes. When taxes weren't paid, the government couldn't function. And when the government couldn't function, the entire system started to break down. While the correlation between low floods and political collapse is strong, we should recognize this as a significant contributing factor rather than the sole cause.

There wasn't a single bad year, but there were inadequate floods over an extended period, possibly linked to broader climate changes affecting northeastern Africa. Some years were probably fine, but others were disastrous, and the uncertainty itself was destabilizing. The Old Kingdom had been built on the assumption of a reliable agricultural surplus. When that surplus became unreliable, everything else became vulnerable.

Second, there was a political problem. The central government had become weaker while regional governors had grown stronger. Throughout the Old Kingdom, pharaohs had appointed governors to manage Egypt's provinces (nomes). These governors, called nomarchs, were initially royal appointees who served at the king's pleasure. But over time, particularly during the long reign of Pepi II, these positions increasingly became hereditary in many regions. Nomarchs passed their offices to their sons, creating regional dynasties with their own power bases.

These hereditary nomarchs built their own tombs in their home provinces rather than near the royal pyramid, suggesting they identified more with their region than with the king. They maintained their own courts, officials, and military forces. Gradually, they became semi-independent rulers who happened to acknowledge the distant pharaoh's authority—when it was convenient.

Third, there was an economic crisis tied to how the Old Kingdom government had operated. The pharaohs had granted extensive lands and resources to temples and to support the mortuary cults of deceased kings. These grants were permanent; once they were given, they couldn't easily be taken back. Over generations, more and more of Egypt's productive capacity became locked into these religious endowments, reducing the resources available to the reigning king. While exact figures are debated and difficult to confirm with existing records, scholars suggest that by the late Old Kingdom, a substantial portion of Egypt's agricultural land might have been committed to supporting temples and deceased kings' cults, leaving current pharaohs with shrinking revenue bases.

Fourth, there might have been a succession crisis. After Pepi II's incredibly long reign, the succession became murky. Several short reigns followed, suggesting instability in the royal family. When multiple claimants compete for the throne or when kings die quickly one after another, it undermines the entire system. Regional officials don't know who to support. The administration becomes paralyzed, and authority fragments.

The Seventh and Eighth Dynasties, which followed immediately after the Sixth, are not well known. Later Egyptian tradition claimed the Seventh Dynasty consisted of "seventy kings in seventy days." That is obviously not literally true, but it does indicate chaos and rapid turnover. The Eighth Dynasty kings seem to have been legitimate heirs to the Sixth Dynasty throne, ruling from Memphis, but their authority was limited, and their reigns were short.

By around 2160 BCE, Egypt had effectively split into competing power centers. The traditional capital at Memphis maintained some kings who claimed to rule all Egypt, but their actual control probably extended only over the immediate region. Meanwhile, powerful nomarch families in places like Herakleopolis in Middle Egypt and Thebes in Upper Egypt were establishing their own mini-kingdoms, paying lip service to Memphis while acting independently.

The Ninth and Tenth Dynasties, centered at Herakleopolis, represent one of these rival power centers. The Herakleopolitan kings controlled Middle Egypt and parts of the delta, and they claimed to be the legitimate rulers of Egypt. However, their authority was contested, particularly by an emerging power farther south: Thebes.

The Eleventh Dynasty, which would eventually reunify Egypt, started as just another provincial power based in Thebes in Upper Egypt. Initially, these Theban rulers were simply local strongmen controlling a few nomes around Thebes. But unlike many regional rulers who were content with local power, the Thebans had ambitions to control all of Egypt.

The result was civil war or at least prolonged conflict with Herakleopolis. This conflict played out over decades, with neither side strong enough to decisively defeat the other.

Life in a Fractured Land

What was this fragmented Egypt actually like? The sources are frustratingly limited, but we can sketch an outline.

Central authority had collapsed, but Egypt hadn't descended into complete anarchy. Instead, it had fractured into a patchwork of competing regional powers. Each nome or group of nomes was governed by local strongmen—sometimes hereditary nomarchs from Old Kingdom families, sometimes new men who had seized power. These local rulers maintained order in their territories, collected taxes, administered justice, and sometimes fought with their neighbors over borders and resources.

Some nomes prospered under capable local rulers who weren't sending tribute to a distant capital. Others suffered under weak or exploitative leaders, or they became battlegrounds as competing powers fought for control. The experience varied greatly depending on where you lived and who ruled your region.

Trade and communication between regions became more difficult and fragmented. The unified economic system of the Old Kingdom, where goods and resources flowed freely along the Nile under royal authority, had fractured. Now, goods had to pass through multiple territories, each controlled by different rulers who might demand tolls or simply block passage. While some trade continued, particularly at local and regional levels, the barriers created by political fragmentation reduced the ease and volume of long-distance commerce.

Security deteriorated in some areas. Without a strong central authority, banditry increased. Desert nomads, who had been kept in check during the Old Kingdom by Egyptian military power, raided into the Nile Valley. Some texts from this period speak of famine, social disorder, and the breakdown of traditional hierarchies.

However, we need to be careful about how we interpret these sources. Many of the texts describing chaos and disaster were written by scribes lamenting the loss of the old order and its certainties. These weren't necessarily true descriptions of the current conditions; they were often political propaganda designed to justify the need for strong central authority or nostalgic texts idealizing the past. The reality was probably less universally terrible than these texts suggest, even if it was certainly harder for many people than the stable Old Kingdom had been.

In regions with stable local governance, life probably continued much as it had during the Old Kingdom. You worked, paid taxes to your local lord instead of a distant pharaoh, participated in local festivals, and hoped for a good flood. Local markets functioned. Trade still occurred, though perhaps on a more limited scale. Social hierarchies persisted, though with more fluidity than in the rigid Old Kingdom system.

In less stable regions, survival became harder. When fighting broke out between rival powers, crops might be destroyed, irrigation systems damaged, and villages pillaged. When the Nile floods were poor and there was no centralized grain storage system to provide relief, local famines could be devastating. Archaeological evidence of widespread famine remains uneven across regions, suggesting that suffering was likely concentrated in specific regions and times rather than occurring throughout Egypt.

Some texts mention people selling themselves or their children into servitude to avoid starvation. Other texts describe abandoned settlements and empty fields, suggesting population decline in some regions due to death or migration.

Archaeological evidence suggests that many settlements continued functioning throughout the First Intermediate Period. Craft production continued. Local temples were maintained and sometimes expanded. New tombs were built for local elites. None of this would be happening if conditions were uniformly catastrophic.

One interesting development was increased mobility. When the central authority collapsed, people could move more easily between regions to seek better conditions. If one nomarch was oppressive or if harvests failed in one region, people could migrate to areas with better governance or more food. This was harder to do during the Old Kingdom when the state controlled movement more strictly.

The First Intermediate Period also saw changes in military organization. The large-scale royal armies of the Old Kingdom had been disbanded. Instead, local rulers maintained smaller military forces, such as personal retinues, local militias, and hired troops. This created opportunities for military careers that hadn't existed before. A capable fighter could rise in the service of a local nomarch, potentially achieving status that would have been impossible in the rigid Old Kingdom hierarchy.

For the average Egyptian farmer, the collapse of central authority might not have changed daily life as dramatically as we might think. You still worked your fields, paid your taxes (now to a local ruler instead of a distant king), and worried about the harvest. The pharaoh had always been a remote figure; now he was even more remote. As long as your immediate region was stable and well governed, life could go on much as it had before.

But the psychological impact was real. The Old Kingdom had seemed everlasting, built on cosmic principles that the pharaoh maintained through his divine nature. When that system collapsed, it must have shaken people's fundamental understanding of how the world worked. If ma'at could fail, if the eternal order could break down, what did that mean?

Religious life adapted to the changed circumstances. The great royal mortuary temples and pyramid complexes of the Old Kingdom had been supported by permanent endowments of land and resources. When the central authority collapsed, maintaining these temples became difficult. Some were abandoned, while others were maintained with reduced resources.

However, local temples often flourished. Without needing to send resources to support royal cult centers, local communities could invest more in their own temples. Provincial gods gained more importance. This religious decentralization would have lasting effects on the Egyptian religion.

Culture in a Fragmented Age

Historians used to call the First Intermediate Period a "dark age"—a time of chaos, poverty, and cultural decline between two golden ages. Modern scholars have become more skeptical of this characterization. Yes, central authority collapsed, and records became scarcer, but does that necessarily mean the period was uniformly terrible? Or were different things happening, things that don't show up as clearly in the archaeological record?

The term "dark age" suggests a period we know little about because few texts and monuments survived. This is partly true for the First Intermediate Period—we have fewer royal inscriptions, fewer dated monuments, and less certainty about the exact sequence of rulers. The archaeological record becomes harder to interpret when you don't have a strong centralized authority producing standardized records and monuments.

But "dark age" also implies cultural decline and social misery, and that's where modern scholars have started to push back. The First

Intermediate Period looks dark compared to the Old Kingdom, partly because we're looking for the wrong things. We're looking for pyramids, royal inscriptions, and evidence of a centralized administration. When we don't find them, we assume everything collapsed. But maybe Egypt was just organized differently, and cultural production was happening at regional levels.

Political organization had clearly changed. Instead of a single strong pharaoh controlling all Egypt from Memphis, power was dispersed among multiple rulers. These competing rulers fought each other, but they also governed. The system was messier and more fragmented than the Old Kingdom, but it wasn't complete chaos.

In fact, in some regions, evidence suggests areas might have benefited from the collapse of central authority. During the Old Kingdom, provincial resources had been extracted to support the king's building projects and the royal court in Memphis. Now, in areas where capable local rulers emerged, those resources could stay local. A capable nomarch could use local wealth to improve irrigation systems, build local temples, support local craftsmen, and generally benefit his region rather than enriching a distant capital.

The archaeological evidence supports this. We see substantial tomb construction continuing throughout the First Intermediate Period, but it happened in the provinces rather than near Memphis. Nomarchs built elaborate rock-cut tombs in their home territories—places like Beni Hasan, Asyut, and Thebes. These tombs were sometimes quite sophisticated, decorated with painted scenes showing local life, religious rituals, and the nomarch's achievements.

Unlike the pyramids and mastabas of the Old Kingdom, these tombs were carved directly into cliff faces. This was partly practical—stone was harder to transport when the central authority had collapsed—but it also created different architectural possibilities.

The tomb of Ankhtifi at el-Mo'alla, for example, contains biographical inscriptions describing how this nomarch maintained order in his region during a time of crisis: "I gave bread to the hungry and clothing to the naked; I brought the cattle of the herdsman to high ground ... There was no one dying of hunger in my time."

Whether Ankhtifi actually did all this is not as important as what the inscription reveals: even local strongmen felt the need to justify their rule by claiming to maintain ma'at and care for their people. The ideology of good governance persisted even when centralized kingship had collapsed.

The art style in these provincial tombs differs from Old Kingdom art. It's less standardized, more varied, and sometimes less technically accomplished but often more lively and creative. Provincial artists weren't following strict royal artistic conventions; they were developing their own regional styles. This produced art that's rougher in execution but sometimes more interesting and experimental. It was less bound by tradition.

Some scholars argue this shows artistic decline since provincial artists lacked the skill of royal workshops. Others argue it represents artistic freedom; without royal standards to follow, artists could innovate. The truth is probably somewhere in between. Technical skills might have declined in some places when royal workshops closed and master craftsmen weren't training apprentices in the old methods. However, regional styles could flourish because artists weren't constrained by the central authority.

Stelae (stone slabs with inscriptions) from this period also show stylistic changes. Many are roughly carved compared to Old Kingdom standards, but they're also more numerous and more widely distributed. Non-elite individuals could afford commemorative stelae that would have been beyond their means or access during the Old Kingdom. This suggests either that costs had decreased with the collapse of royal workshops or that wealth had been redistributed—or both.

Pottery from the First Intermediate Period also shows regional variation. Without standardized royal pottery workshops, local potters developed distinctive regional styles. Archaeologists can identify where pottery was made based on these regional characteristics, which helps us understand trade patterns and regional interactions during this period.

Literature, interestingly, seems to have flourished during the First Intermediate Period. Some of ancient Egypt's most famous literary texts either come from this period or reflect on it. These include texts lamenting social disorder, instructions on how to behave morally, and reflections on mortality and the meaning of life. The literature of this period reflects genuine anxiety about social disorder, reversed hierarchies, and the absence of strong kingship.

The *Admonitions of Ipuwer* describes a world turned upside down: "Indeed, the land turns around as does a potter's wheel. The robber is now a possessor of riches ... Indeed, noble ladies are gleaners, and nobles are in the workhouse." The text depicts complete social inversion—the wealthy are reduced to poverty, the poor are enriched, and traditional hierarchies have collapsed.

Is this description accurate? Probably not literally. It's likely a literary exaggeration designed to emphasize how far Egypt had fallen from the ideal order, and it might reflect retrospective anxieties about the period rather than providing a report of actual conditions. However, it reveals what Egyptians feared most: not just poverty or violence but the collapse of the social order itself.

The *Instructions for Merikare* takes a different approach. This text, supposedly written by a Herakleopolitan king to his son, provides advice on how to rule: be just, reward competent officials, maintain the borders, care for the welfare of your people, and respect the gods. But it also acknowledges hard realities: "A generation of people passes by, and the gods who were aforetime rest in their pyramids ... Be not evil. Patience is good. Make your monument last through love of you."

This text shows a ruler trying to navigate difficult times, acknowledging that even kings are mortal and that good governance requires more than divine authority. It also requires competence, justice, and earning people's loyalty. It's more pragmatic and less triumphant than Old Kingdom royal ideology.

The *Dispute Between a Man and His Ba* is even more philosophical. In this text, a man debates with his ba (his soul or spiritual essence) about whether life is worth living. The man wants to die and enter the afterlife, but his ba argues for staying alive. The text includes beautiful poetry: "Death is before me today like the recovery of a sick man, like going forth into a garden after sickness. Death is before me today like the odor of myrrh, like sitting under the sail on a windy day." This text shows Egyptians grappling with existential questions about meaning, mortality, and the value of life in difficult times.

By around 2055 BCE, after more than a century of fragmentation, Egypt was ready for reunification. The Theban rulers of the Eleventh Dynasty had gradually extended their control northward, conquering or absorbing rival territories. The Herakleopolitan kingdom had weakened. The stage was set for a Theban king to reunify all of Egypt and establish the Middle Kingdom.

The First Intermediate Period showed that Egyptian civilization was resilient—it survived the collapse of central authority, after all—but also that it deeply valued unified kingship. The disorder of this period would make Egyptians appreciate centralized rule even more when it was eventually restored. The Middle Kingdom that followed would be built on lessons learned during the collapse: the importance of strong but just kingship, the value of provincial loyalty, the need for competent administration, and the dangers of letting royal authority erode.

Chapter 5: The Middle Kingdom — Reunification and Renaissance

Egypt Reunited

Around 2055 BCE, a Theban king named Mentuhotep II achieved what had seemed impossible for over a century: he reunified Egypt. (Scholarly estimates for this reunification vary, with some placing it closer to 2040 BCE, but we'll use the commonly cited date of around 2055 BCE throughout this book.) The First Intermediate Period ended not with a peaceful agreement but with conquest, as the Theban rulers of Upper Egypt defeated their rivals in the north and brought the entire Nile Valley back under a single ruler's control.

Mentuhotep II (who reigned approximately 2055 to 2004 BCE) was the second king of the Eleventh Dynasty to bear that name, but he was the first to control all of Egypt. His predecessors had ruled only the Theban region of Upper Egypt, locked in a long conflict with the Herakleopolitan kings who controlled Middle and Lower Egypt. This civil war had dragged on for decades, with neither side able to deliver a decisive blow.

Mentuhotep II seems to have been both a capable military leader and an effective administrator. He extended Theban control northward, conquering or absorbing territories one by one. The details are frustratingly sparse—we don't have detailed battle accounts or campaign records—but the result is clear. By around 2055 BCE, the Herakleopolitan kingdom had fallen, and Mentuhotep II claimed control over Egypt from the First Cataract in the south to the Mediterranean in the north, though full administrative control over the entire territory, particularly in the delta and northern regions, would have taken time to establish completely.

Reunification required more than military victory; it required convincing provincial rulers throughout Egypt to accept Theban authority. Mentuhotep had to rebuild administrative systems that had fragmented and restore confidence in centralized kingship. The king adopted an epithet to mark the reunification: "Sematowy," meaning "Uniter of the Two Lands." This wasn't just propaganda. Mentuhotep II presented himself as restoring ma'at, bringing back the proper order that had been lost during the chaos of the First Intermediate Period. He was, in a sense, Egypt's second founder, completing what Narmer had done hundreds of years earlier.

Thebes now became Egypt's capital. This represented a significant shift. During the Old Kingdom, Memphis had been the undisputed center of power. During the First Intermediate Period, power had been dispersed among multiple centers. Now, Thebes in Upper Egypt became the royal residence and primary administrative center, though Memphis retained importance as a traditional power center and religious site.

The choice of Thebes had lasting consequences. It elevated the city's patron god, Amun, to national prominence. While Amun had existed as a god during the Old Kingdom, he was relatively minor compared to major state deities. Now, as the god of Egypt's new ruling dynasty, Amun's cult would grow dramatically in wealth and influence, eventually making him the king of the Egyptian gods. The priests of Amun at Thebes would become some of the most powerful people in Egypt.

Mentuhotep II ruled for over fifty years, giving Egypt the stability it desperately needed. However, the Eleventh Dynasty would be short-lived. His successors—Mentuhotep III and Mentuhotep IV—ruled for relatively brief periods. Then, around 1985 BCE, power passed to a new dynasty, the Twelfth, though the transition seems to have been peaceful.

The first king of the Twelfth Dynasty, Amenemhat I (approximately 1985–1956 BCE), might have been Mentuhotep IV's vizier, who took the throne possibly through a coup. Ancient sources hint at irregularities in the succession, and later literature would justify Amenemhat I's rule by emphasizing the need for strong leadership. A text called the *Prophecy of Neferti* (written after the fact, despite its supposed predictive nature) described the chaos of the First Intermediate Period and prophesied the coming of a king named Ameny (short for Amenemhat) who would restore order. This was propaganda designed to legitimize the new dynasty.

Amenemhat I made the crucial decision to move the capital north from Thebes to a new city called Itjtawy, located near the Faiyum region in Middle Egypt. This was strategic. While Thebes was important as the dynasty's ancestral home and as a religious center for Amun, it was far south, making the administration of Lower Egypt difficult. Itjtawy, positioned between Upper and Lower Egypt, could serve as a better administrative center for the kingdom.

This didn't diminish Thebes—the city remained extremely important, and Amun remained the state god—but it showed pragmatic thinking about governance. The Twelfth Dynasty kings would be buried near their new capital, not at Thebes, though they continued to build temples and monuments at Thebes.

Amenemhat I also established a practice that would become characteristic of the Middle Kingdom: co-regency. Near the end of his reign, he elevated his son Senusret I as co-ruler, allowing for a smooth transition of power. When Amenemhat I died—according to later literature, specifically the *Teaching of Amenemhat*, he was assassinated in a palace conspiracy—Senusret I was already established as king and could take full power immediately.

The *Teaching of Amenemhat* is a remarkable text. It was supposedly written by the dead king to his son, warning him about the dangers of court life: "Trust not a brother, know not a friend, make not for yourself intimates—there is no fulfilling of the heart in them." Whether this literary text reflects an actual assassination or was composed to explain a succession crisis and justify Senusret I's rule is uncertain, but either way, it shows the political dangers that even powerful kings faced or that later propagandists wanted people to believe they faced.

Senusret I (approximately 1956-1911 BCE) inherited a stable Egypt and spent his long reign strengthening it further. The Twelfth Dynasty continued with a succession of capable rulers: Amenemhat II, Senusret II, Senusret III, and Amenemhat III. Each contributed to Egypt's prosperity and power, though Senusret III and Amenemhat III particularly stand out.

Senusret III (approximately 1870-1831 BCE) was one of the Middle Kingdom's greatest military leaders. Perhaps more importantly, he undertook significant administrative reforms. Evidence suggests he substantially weakened or reorganized the system of hereditary nomarchs who had become so powerful during the First Intermediate Period. By the end of his reign, the old nome system had been reorganized, with many nomarchs apparently replaced by royal appointees who could be transferred and dismissed. This centralized royal power in a way that hadn't existed since the Old Kingdom.

Amenemhat III (approximately 1831–1786 BCE) presided over what was probably the Middle Kingdom's economic peak. His long reign was peaceful and prosperous. He focused on internal development, particularly large-scale irrigation and reclamation projects in the Faiyum region, turning marshland into productive agricultural land. He exploited the mineral resources of the Sinai and the eastern desert. His reign represents the Middle Kingdom at its most successful—a stable, wealthy, well-administered kingdom under a strong pharaoh.

But the dynasty's end was messy. Amenemhat III was succeeded by Amenemhat IV and then by Queen Sobekneferu, Egypt's first clearly attested female ruler. Sobekneferu's reign was brief—only about four years—and ended without an obvious heir, leading to the end of the Twelfth Dynasty around 1802 BCE.

The Thirteenth Dynasty followed, but it never achieved the stability of the Twelfth. Kings succeeded each other rapidly, suggesting political instability or short reigns for unknown reasons. Egypt remained unified and relatively prosperous during the early Thirteenth Dynasty, but the rapid turnover of rulers indicated underlying problems. The strong centralized state that Mentuhotep II had rebuilt and that the Twelfth Dynasty had perfected was beginning to weaken again.

The Golden Age of Literature and Art

The Middle Kingdom produced some of ancient Egypt's greatest literary works and most beautiful art. Modern scholars often call the Middle Kingdom the "classical age" of Egyptian culture, when the Egyptian language and artistic traditions reached a level of sophistication that later periods would try to imitate.

The language itself is telling. Middle Egyptian, the form of the language used during this period, became the standard "classical" Egyptian that scribes would continue to use for formal inscriptions for over a thousand years, even after the spoken language had evolved into later forms. When you see hieroglyphic inscriptions from the New Kingdom or even the Late Period, they're often written in Middle Egyptian rather than the contemporary language, much like Latin continued to be used for formal documents in medieval Europe long after people stopped speaking it daily.

The Old Kingdom had produced practical texts, like administrative records, royal inscriptions, and religious spells, but relatively little that we'd recognize as literature. The First Intermediate Period had produced some notable works, but they were mostly focused on the crisis of the time. The Middle Kingdom produced a diverse range of literary genres: adventure stories, moral instructions, religious hymns, love poetry, and philosophical dialogues.

The *Tale of Sinuhe* is perhaps the Middle Kingdom's most famous literary work, and it's genuinely good literature by any standard. The story follows Sinuhe, a royal courtier who overhears news of King Amenemhat I's assassination. Fearing he might be implicated, Sinuhe flees Egypt in a panic. He becomes a refugee in Syria, where he rises to become a powerful chief, marries, has children, and leads a successful life. But he never stops longing for Egypt. In his old age, the new pharaoh (Senusret I) invites him home, and Sinuhe returns to Egypt, where he's welcomed and given a proper tomb so he can be buried in his homeland.

The story explores themes of identity, belonging, fear, exile, and redemption. Sinuhe's internal conflict—his success abroad versus his desperate longing for home—feels real. The story doesn't have simple heroes or villains; it has complex characters making understandable choices. The prose is elegant, with vivid descriptions and emotional depth.

The *Eloquent Peasant* is another masterpiece, telling the story of a peasant named Khun-Anup whose goods are stolen by a corrupt official. Seeking justice, the peasant appeals to the local magistrate with a series of elaborate, eloquent speeches about justice, righteousness, and the duties of officials. The magistrate is so impressed by the peasant's eloquence that he keeps delaying judgment just to hear more speeches. Eventually, justice is done—the peasant gets his goods back, and the corrupt official is punished.

The story works on multiple levels. It's entertaining; the peasant's increasingly frustrated eloquence is genuinely witty. It's also a meditation on justice and the moral obligations of those in power. The speeches are beautiful examples of Egyptian rhetoric, filled with metaphors and wordplay. And there's an underlying tension. The magistrate's delay means justice is slow, even when the powerful find the petitioner amusing. Is this really how justice should work?

The "Instructions" genre continued from earlier periods but reached new heights. The *Instructions of Ptahhotep* (possibly from the Old Kingdom but preserved in Middle Kingdom copies) offered advice on proper behavior and wisdom. These texts weren't just lists of rules; they were also thoughtful explorations of how to live well and govern justly.

Religious literature also flourished. Hymns to various gods were composed with poetic beauty. The "Hymn to the Nile" celebrated the river that made Egypt possible: "Hail to you, O Nile, who manifest yourself over this land and come in peace to give life to Egypt." The "Hymn to Senusret III" praised the king but in ways that revealed what Egyptians valued in their rulers: "How the gods rejoice—you have strengthened their offerings. How the people rejoice—you have established their frontiers. How your forebears rejoice—you have increased their portions."

The Coffin Texts, religious spells that had democratized in the First Intermediate Period, were further developed and standardized in the Middle Kingdom. These spells, painted on coffins, were meant to help the deceased navigate the afterlife. They show complex religious thinking about death, the soul, and eternal life.

Art during the Middle Kingdom showed distinctive characteristics. Sculpture achieved a level of realism and psychological depth that was new. The famous statues of Senusret III don't show a generic divine king. They show a specific individual with prominent ears and a serious, almost brooding expression. Some scholars interpret these portraits as showing realistic age and personality. Others argue they're still idealized but representing a new ideal: the king as experienced, serious, burdened by responsibility rather than eternally youthful and triumphant. Either way, they're psychologically complex in a way Old Kingdom royal sculpture rarely was.

Statues of Senusret III.'

Private sculptures—statues of non-royal individuals—also flourished. These ranged from traditional standing or seated figures to "block statues," showing a man squatting with his knees drawn up and his body wrapped in a cloak, creating a compact block shape. These block statues would remain popular throughout Egyptian history.

Jewelry from the Middle Kingdom is spectacular. Egyptian craftsmen had always been skilled in metalwork, but Middle Kingdom jewelry shows great refinement. The treasures found in the tombs of Middle Kingdom princesses—intricately designed pectorals inlaid with semi-precious stones, delicate beadwork, and elaborate diadems—demonstrate extraordinary technical skill and artistic sophistication.

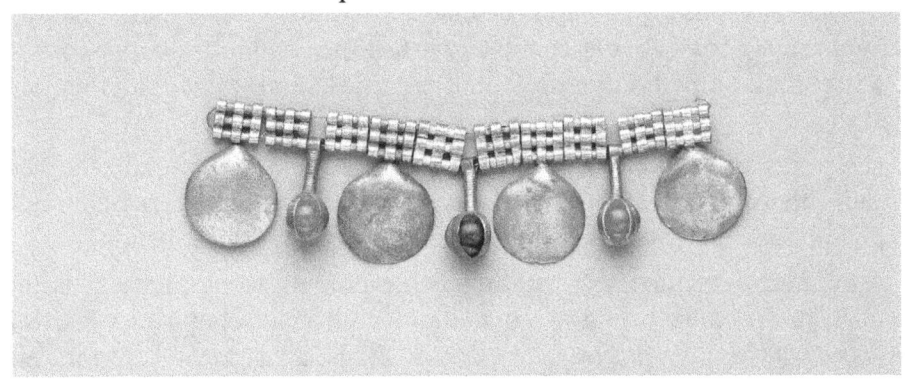

Jewelry from the Middle Kingdom'

Architecture during the Middle Kingdom shifted away from the massive pyramids of the Old Kingdom. Kings still built pyramids, but they were smaller and often built with a mudbrick core rather than solid stone. The Middle Kingdom pyramids also don't match their Old Kingdom predecessors in scale or durability (many have collapsed or are poorly eroded), but the pyramid complexes included elaborate temples and tombs.

The mortuary temple of Mentuhotep II at Deir el-Bahri is particularly notable. It is a terraced structure built against the cliff face. This temple inspired one of ancient Egypt's most famous buildings: Queen Hatshepsut's mortuary temple, built right next to it about five hundred years later.

Rock-cut tombs became more elaborate. At Beni Hasan in Middle Egypt, provincial officials carved tombs into the cliffs with painted columns, decorated chapels, and vivid scenes of daily life. These tombs show the wealth and power of even provincial elites during the Middle Kingdom's prosperous years.

Why did the Middle Kingdom produce such a remarkable culture? Stability and prosperity provided the resources and leisure for cultural production. When society is stable and wealthy, it can support artists, poets, and scribes who have time to refine their crafts.

The experience of the First Intermediate Period also forced Egyptians to think deeply about their society, values, and system of government. Literature from this period shows more questioning, more philosophical reflection, and more interest in individual psychology and moral complexity than earlier periods. The breakdown and restoration of order had made Egyptians more conscious of what they valued and why.

Royal patronage encouraged culture. Middle Kingdom pharaohs supported scribal schools, temple workshops, and artistic production. They commissioned literature, built libraries, and valued literacy and learning.

The spread of literacy, which was still limited to a small elite but broader than before, created audiences for literature. More people could read and appreciate texts, creating a market for literary production.

The Middle Kingdom's cultural achievements would have a lasting impact. Its literature would be copied and studied for centuries. Its artistic styles would be imitated by later periods. Its language would become the classical standard. When New Kingdom Egyptians wanted to connect with their glorious past, they looked back to the Middle Kingdom as a golden age of culture and wisdom.

Expansion and Fortification

The Middle Kingdom wasn't just an age of cultural achievement. It was also an age of military expansion and strategic defense. The Twelfth Dynasty pharaohs, particularly Senusret I, Senusret III, and Amenemhat III, pushed Egypt's borders farther than they'd been since the Old Kingdom, established firm control over Nubia to the south, and created defensive systems to protect Egyptian interests.

Nubia was the primary target of Middle Kingdom expansion. This region, stretching south from Egypt's traditional border at the First Cataract, was rich in resources that Egypt desperately wanted: gold, copper, semi-precious stones, exotic wood, ivory, and access to trade routes reaching deep into Africa. During the Old Kingdom, Egypt conducted expeditions into Nubia and maintained trading relationships with the Nubians. During the First Intermediate Period, Egyptian control collapsed, and Nubia became independent.

The Middle Kingdom pharaohs were determined to reassert Egyptian dominance. Senusret I conducted military campaigns into Lower Nubia, the region immediately south of Egypt. He erected a stela at Buhen near the Second Cataract claiming to have established Egypt's border there. However, claiming territory and actually controlling it are different things.

Senusret III took the Nubian conquest to a new level. He conducted at least three major campaigns into Nubia during his reign, pushing Egyptian control firmly to the Second Cataract and beyond. His inscriptions describe these campaigns with unusual frankness about the difficulties involved. One boundary stela erected during his eighth regnal year states: "Southern boundary, made in year 8, under the majesty of the King ... in order to prevent any Nubian from crossing it, by water or by land, with a ship or any herds of the Nubians; except a Nubian who shall come to do trading ... or with a commission. Every good thing shall be done with them, but without allowing a ship of the Nubians to pass ... downstream, forever."

This was a controlled occupation with regulations about trade and movement. Nubians weren't banned entirely; they could trade at Egyptian outposts and pass with permission. However, unauthorized movement across the border was forbidden.

To maintain control, the Middle Kingdom established an elaborate system of fortifications in Nubia. Between the First and Second Cataracts, at least thirteen major forts were built, mostly during the reign of Senusret III. These were substantial military installations with massive mudbrick walls, ditches, bastions, and sophisticated defensive features.

Some of these forts were enormous. The fort at Buhen had walls over thirty feet high and sixteen feet thick, with towers projecting from the walls to allow defenders to fire on attackers from multiple angles. The fort at Semna controlled a narrow passage in the Nile where all boat traffic had to pass. The fort at Mirgissa included not just fortifications but also workshops, granaries, administrative buildings, and housing for the garrison and their families.

These forts served multiple purposes. Militarily, they protected Egypt from Nubian raids and provided bases for Egyptian expeditions farther south. Economically, they controlled trade routes and access to gold mines. Administratively, they extended Egyptian governance into Nubia, with Egyptian officials collecting taxes and enforcing Egyptian law. The forts also served as centers for trade, where Nubians could exchange goods under Egyptian supervision.

The extent and sophistication of these fortifications are remarkable. They show advanced military engineering, with walls designed to resist both direct assaults and siege warfare. They had features like glacis (sloped walls) to prevent mining, dry moats, and carefully planned fields of fire. They also show the Middle Kingdom's administrative capacity. Building and maintaining these forts required organizing labor, transporting supplies, maintaining garrisons, and creating supply chains stretching hundreds of miles from Egypt.

The Middle Kingdom also conducted military operations in the Levant (modern Israel, Palestine, Lebanon, and Syria), though on a smaller scale than in Nubia. Egyptian interest in this region was partly economic—the Levant produced cedar wood, wine, olive oil, and other goods Egypt wanted—and partly strategic, as controlling trade routes through the Levant provided wealth and prevented threats from western Asia.

Evidence for Middle Kingdom activity in the Levant includes Egyptian artifacts found at sites in the region, Egyptian inscriptions mentioning campaigns or expeditions, and references in Egyptian texts to Asian prisoners or tribute. The famous "Execration Texts"—pottery bowls or clay figurines inscribed with the names of Egypt's enemies and then ritually broken—include names of Levantine cities and rulers, showing Egyptian interest in this region.

However, there were no permanent forts or major Egyptian settlements. Instead, Egypt maintained commercial relationships, sometimes backed by military expeditions or threats, with the various city-states of the region. The pharaoh claimed dominance, but actual control was limited.

Trade networks expanded dramatically during the Middle Kingdom. Egyptian expeditions reached Punt (probably somewhere on the Red Sea coast of modern Sudan, Eritrea, or Somalia), bringing back incense, myrrh, ebony, ivory, and exotic animals. Ships traveled to Byblos on the Lebanese coast for cedar. Trade routes connected Egypt with the Aegean world, western Asia, and deep into Africa.

Internally, the Middle Kingdom invested in infrastructure. Irrigation systems were expanded and improved. The Faiyum region, a natural depression west of the Nile, was developed through water management projects that increased agricultural productivity. Canals and water control systems allowed more land to be cultivated.

The Middle Kingdom's expansion and fortification showed Egypt at the height of its power during this period. The kingdom was culturally sophisticated, militarily strong, administratively capable, and economically prosperous. The pharaohs could project power hundreds of miles from Egypt's traditional borders, maintain permanent military installations in conquered territories, and organize complex logistical systems to support expansion.

But this system required a strong central authority. The forts needed to be manned, supplied, and maintained. The administration needed to function smoothly. The pharaoh needed to be effective and respected. When these conditions held, the Middle Kingdom flourished. When they began to break down in the late Thirteenth Dynasty, the entire system became vulnerable.

Chapter 6:
The Second Intermediate Period and the Hyksos

Foreign Rulers on Egyptian Soil

The Second Intermediate Period (approximately 1802-1550 BCE, though scholarly chronologies vary, with some placing the start closer to 1782 or 1750 BCE) was one of ancient Egypt's most dramatic and controversial chapters. For the first time in Egyptian history, Lower Egypt and parts of Middle Egypt fell under the control of foreign rulers—people Egyptians called the Hyksos. This wasn't a brief raid or a temporary occupation. For a period of time (the exact duration is debated among scholars), foreign kings ruled northern Egypt from their capital in the delta, while native Egyptian rulers controlled Upper Egypt from Thebes. Egypt was divided again, but this time, the division wasn't just between competing Egyptian factions. It was between Egyptians and outsiders. The political landscape was complex, with overlapping dynasties, vassal states, and contested buffer regions making the reality more intricate than a simple north-south divide.

Who were the Hyksos? The name comes from the Egyptian phrase *hekau khasut*, which means "rulers of foreign lands" or "foreign chiefs." Later Egyptian propaganda would demonize them as barbaric invaders who conquered Egypt through military force and ruled with cruelty. The reality was more complex.

The Hyksos weren't a single unified people or ethnic group. They were primarily Semitic-speaking peoples from the Levant (the region covering modern Syria, Lebanon, Israel, and Palestine) who had been migrating into the Egyptian delta for generations. During the late Middle Kingdom, particularly during the Thirteenth Dynasty, these migrations increased. Some came as traders, some as laborers, some as mercenaries, and some as refugees fleeing conflicts or famines in their homelands.

This wasn't unusual or alarming at first. Egypt had long maintained contact with neighboring peoples, and foreigners had long settled in Egypt, particularly in the cosmopolitan delta region bordering Asia. Egyptian texts from the Middle Kingdom mention Asian peoples living in Egypt, working in various occupations, and even serving in the Egyptian military.

What changed during the late Thirteenth Dynasty was the weakening of central Egyptian authority. The Thirteenth Dynasty suffered from political instability, with kings succeeding each other rapidly. This created a power vacuum, particularly in the delta, which was far from the Thirteenth Dynasty capital.

Into this vacuum stepped ambitious leaders from the Asiatic communities in the delta. Rather than a single dramatic invasion, the Hyksos takeover was probably gradual. Local strongmen with Asian backgrounds gained control of the delta towns. They established their own power bases, collected taxes, and maintained armies. Eventually, these local rulers united into a kingdom centered at Avaris in the eastern delta. Their leaders declared themselves pharaohs—the Fifteenth Dynasty, ruling approximately 1650 to 1550 BCE.

The Hyksos adopted Egyptian royal titles, used Egyptian administrative systems, wrote their names in hieroglyphs, and presented themselves as legitimate pharaohs. They weren't trying to destroy Egyptian civilization; they were trying to become Egyptian kings. But they still maintained distinctive cultural elements, creating a syncretic hybrid culture at Avaris. They worshiped the Egyptian god Seth (associated with foreign lands and chaos in Egyptian mythology—perhaps an ironic choice, or perhaps they identified with Seth's power and foreignness). They also continued to worship Levantine deities. Archaeological evidence shows substantial Asian cultural elements, including distinctive house styles, burial customs, and pottery types alongside Egyptian forms, demonstrating cultural fusion rather than simple adoption of Egyptian traditions.

Avaris was strategically located in the eastern delta, close to the routes leading to and from the Levant. Archaeological evidence shows that the Hyksos capital was a wealthy, cosmopolitan city. Pottery from Cyprus, the Levant, and Nubia has been found there, indicating extensive trade networks. The city included temples, palaces, and substantial residential areas. This wasn't a military camp or a temporary stronghold; it was the capital of a kingdom that expected to endure.

The extent of Hyksos control is debated. They definitely controlled the delta and possibly parts of Middle Egypt. Upper Egypt, however, remained under the control of native Egyptian rulers based at Thebes—the Sixteenth and Seventeenth Dynasties. Between the Hyksos kingdom in the north and the Theban kingdom in the south lay a buffer zone of smaller kingdoms and local rulers. Some were more aligned with the Hyksos, while others aligned more with Thebes.

The Fourteenth Dynasty, contemporary with and perhaps a vassal of the Fifteenth Dynasty (the Hyksos), controlled parts of the western delta. The Sixteenth Dynasty is less clearly defined. Scholars debate whether this means they were also Hyksos vassals, highly fragmented local rulers in the buffer regions, or native Egyptian rulers in areas between the Hyksos and Theban territories.

These intermediate territories served as buffer zones between the Hyksos and the Thebans, but they also represented opportunities. Both the Hyksos and the Thebans competed for influence over these regions, trying to extend their control or at least ensure these areas didn't support their rivals.

In Upper Egypt, the Seventeenth Dynasty ruled from Thebes, maintaining the traditions of pharaonic kingship and claiming to be the legitimate rulers of all Egypt, even though they controlled only the south. The early Seventeenth Dynasty kings seem to have coexisted with the Hyksos, perhaps acknowledging Hyksos dominance in exchange for being left alone. This was pragmatic but humiliating, and it couldn't last forever.

The Theban kingdom was smaller and probably less wealthy than the Hyksos kingdom. The delta was richer agricultural land and controlled the Mediterranean trade. Thebes, far to the south, had less economic power. However, Thebes had advantages: a strong sense of Egyptian identity and legitimacy, control of the southern trade routes to Nubia (though these were contested), and military traditions. Most importantly, Thebes had the burning desire to expel the foreigners and reunify Egypt under native rule.

This situation was complicated by yet another group: the Nubians to the south. The Kingdom of Kush, centered at Kerma in Nubia, had grown powerful as Egyptian control weakened. During the Middle Kingdom, this region had been under Egyptian control, with Egyptian fortresses dominating the landscape. Now, those fortresses were in Kushite hands. Kush was a powerful kingdom with its own distinct culture, though it was heavily influenced by centuries of contact with Egypt. Kushite rulers built substantial tombs, controlled valuable trade routes to inner Africa, and fielded armies that could threaten Egyptian territory.

The relationship between the Kushites and Hyksos is murky. Egyptian texts, including the Kamose Stela, mention communication between the two kingdoms. That stela describes intercepting a message from a Hyksos king to the king of Kush, which may represent an actual relationship, or it may be Theban propaganda designed to emphasize the threats they faced. Whether or not there was a formal alliance, the Thebans certainly faced pressures from both directions. The exact nature and extent of any Hyksos-Kushite cooperation is speculative, though.

So, what did the Hyksos bring to Egypt? This is where the story gets interesting. Despite later Egyptian propaganda portraying them as destructive invaders, the Hyksos are widely believed to have introduced important military innovations.

Most significantly, the leading hypothesis among scholars is that they popularized and weaponized the horse and chariot in Egypt, though Egypt might have had limited exposure to these technologies prior to or during the early Hyksos period. Horses weren't native to Egypt and weren't clearly used for military purposes during the Old or Middle Kingdoms. The Hyksos, coming from regions where horses had been domesticated and had chariots developed for warfare, very likely brought this military technology to Egypt. The war chariot—a light, fast, two-wheeled vehicle pulled by horses—revolutionized ancient warfare. It provided mobility, speed, and a stable platform for archers.

The Hyksos also introduced or popularized new types of weapons, like the composite bow (made from multiple materials and more powerful than the simple bows Egyptians had used), new bronze-working techniques, and improved body armor. They brought new musical instruments, new pottery styles, and cultural influences from western Asia.

Ironically, when the Egyptians eventually expelled the Hyksos and reunified Egypt, they adopted all of these innovations themselves. The

New Kingdom Egyptian military, which would build an empire larger than anything Egypt had achieved before, would do so using horses, chariots, composite bows, and military tactics learned from or inspired by the Hyksos.

But Egyptians—at least in Thebes—were humiliated by foreign rule over part of their country. Egyptian ideology held that Egypt was the center of creation, the only truly civilized land. Having foreigners rule any part of Egypt violated this worldview.

The Hyksos period would be remembered by later Egyptians as a time of shame and disaster, even though the actual period seems to have been less catastrophic than propaganda suggested.

Life and Culture in a Divided Land

In the Hyksos-controlled delta, life probably continued much as it had during the Middle Kingdom. Farmers farmed, craftsmen worked, and trade flourished. The main difference was that the rulers had foreign origins and foreign names, and the god Seth received more prominence. For most ordinary Egyptians in the delta, the difference between a native Egyptian pharaoh and a Hyksos pharaoh might not have been enormous. Trade continued. Culture developed. Life went on for most Egyptians.

In the Theban kingdom, there was probably more awareness of and resentment toward the division. The Theban rulers maintained a strong Egyptian identity and claimed to be the legitimate rulers of all Egypt. Royal propaganda emphasized the need to restore ma'at and expel the foreigners. This created a militarized society with a mission.

In the buffer zones of Middle Egypt, life was probably less stable. These regions were contested territory, where power could shift between Hyksos influence, Theban influence, and local autonomy. This created opportunities for ambitious local leaders and dangers, from shifting political allegiances and possible conflict.

Cultural production during the Second Intermediate Period continued, though on a smaller scale than during the unified Middle Kingdom. The Hyksos patronized Egyptian artistic traditions while also introducing Asian elements. Scarabs (seal amulets) from the Hyksos period show both Egyptian and Asian motifs. Pottery styles show mixing of Egyptian and Levantine traditions.

A scarab with the cartouche (an oval frame with the name of an Egyptian pharaoh inside) of a Hyksos king.[10]

In Thebes, artistic production maintained conservative Egyptian traditions, emphasizing continuity with the Middle Kingdom and rejecting foreign influences. Theban art from this period looks deliberately old-fashioned, as if asserting, "We are the true Egyptians, maintaining our traditions, while the north has been corrupted by foreigners."

The religious landscape also shifted. In the Hyksos kingdom, Seth became prominent as the patron deity of the ruling dynasty. In Thebes, Amun continued his rise to supreme importance. The religious division reinforced the political division, as there were different gods for different kingdoms.

Military technology evolved during this period, driven by competition between the kingdoms. The Hyksos' superior military technology—horses, chariots, and composite bows—gave them significant advantages. However, the Thebans were learning and adapting. By the late Second Intermediate Period, the Theban kings had begun acquiring horses and chariots, learning to use these new weapons, and developing tactics to counter them.

By the mid-16th century BCE, the situation was becoming untenable from the Theban perspective. The Seventeenth Dynasty kings, particularly Seqenenre Tao and his sons Kamose and Ahmose, would decide that coexistence with the Hyksos was no longer acceptable. They launched a war to expel the foreigners and reunify Egypt.

This wasn't just about reclaiming territory—it was about restoring Egyptian pride, reasserting the proper cosmic order, and proving that native Egyptian rulers could triumph over foreign invaders. The struggle would be difficult, spanning multiple reigns and requiring fundamental changes in Egyptian military organization and tactics.

But when the war finally succeeded, Egypt wouldn't just return to what it had been during the Middle Kingdom. The experience of fighting the Hyksos, the adoption of new military technologies, the militarization of Egyptian society, renewed economic prosperity, religious developments centered on Amun, and the consolidation of the Theban state would all come together to transform Egypt into something new. It would become an aggressive, expansionist empire that would dominate the Near East for centuries. The New Kingdom was about to begin, born from multiple factors, with the struggle against the Hyksos as the catalyst.

Chapter 7: The New Kingdom Begins—Egypt Becomes a Superpower

Throwing Out the Foreigners

The war that would reunify Egypt and establish the New Kingdom began not with careful planning but with frustration and rage. By the mid-16th century BCE, the Theban rulers of the Seventeenth Dynasty had endured Hyksos domination for generations. They paid tribute, acknowledged Hyksos superiority, and kept their ambitions confined to Upper Egypt. But this humiliating arrangement couldn't last forever.

The decisive break came during the reign of Seqenenre Tao (approximately 1560 BCE), one of the last kings of the Seventeenth Dynasty. Egyptian texts tell a story (almost certainly legendary or symbolic rather than factual, but it perhaps contains a kernel of historical accuracy) about what sparked the conflict. The Hyksos king, Apepi, sent a message to Seqenenre complaining that the hippopotamuses in the sacred pool at Thebes were making so much noise that he couldn't sleep—he lived in Avaris, hundreds of miles to the north. This was obviously a deliberate provocation designed to humiliate the Theban king.

Whether this particular story reflects actual events or not, something triggered open warfare. Seqenenre Tao went to war against the Hyksos. We know this because we have his mummy, and it tells a brutal story. Seqenenre's skull shows multiple severe head wounds from axes and maces, wounds consistent with battlefield trauma. He died violently, probably in battle against the Hyksos or their allies. The war had begun, but the Theban king had paid the ultimate price.

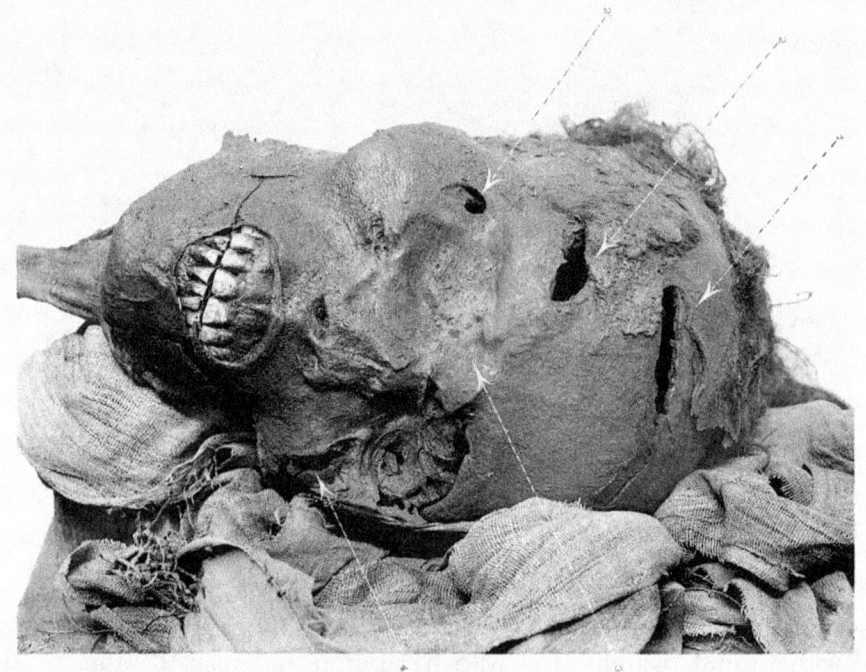

The mummified head of Seqenenre Tao.[ii]

Seqenenre's sons continued the struggle. Kamose, who succeeded his father, was determined to complete what Seqenenre had started. We have two stelae that Kamose erected at Karnak Temple in Thebes, describing his campaigns against the Hyksos.

Kamose's stelae describe his frustration at the divided state of Egypt: "I should like to know what use is my strength, when one ruler is in Avaris and another is in Kush, and I sit united with an Asiatic and a Nubian, each man in possession of his slice of Egypt." He saw himself trapped between enemies, controlling only the middle portion of the Nile Valley, while foreigners ruled both the north and the south.

Kamose describes attacking Hyksos territory, capturing towns, and destroying fields. One dramatic passage describes finding and capturing a Hyksos messenger traveling south with a letter from the Hyksos king to the king of Kush, proposing they coordinate their attacks on Thebes. However, this could have been Theban propaganda to justify the war.

Kamose pushed north, reaching the outskirts of Avaris itself. He describes besieging Hyksos strongholds and celebrating victories. But he didn't complete the conquest. Kamose's reign appears to have been relatively brief. He died before the full expulsion of the Hyksos. The war would fall to the next ruler to finish.

That successor was Ahmose I (approximately 1550-1525 BCE), who might have been Kamose's brother or possibly his son. Ahmose would become the founder of the Eighteenth Dynasty and the New Kingdom, though whether he thought of himself as starting a new era, we cannot know. From his perspective, he was likely continuing his family's war to reunify Egypt and expel the foreigners.

Ahmose spent years fighting the Hyksos. The details are frustratingly sparse. We have fragments of information from various sources but no comprehensive account of the war. What we do know comes from biographical inscriptions of soldiers who served under Ahmose, most notably a soldier also named Ahmose, son of Ebana, whose tomb inscription describes his military career.

Ahmose, son of Ebana, describes multiple campaigns. He fought in battles for control of cities in Middle Egypt. He participated in the siege of Avaris, describing at least three separate assaults on the Hyksos capital. He fought in battles in southern Palestine, pursuing Hyksos forces or allies who had fled Egypt.

Eventually, through persistence, military skill, and probably growing advantages in military technology as the Egyptians learned to use horses and chariots effectively, Ahmose succeeded. Avaris fell, and the Hyksos were expelled from Egypt. Ahmose pursued them into southern Palestine, besieging the town of Sharuhen for three years to eliminate the Hyksos as a military threat even beyond Egypt's borders.

However, the war wasn't finished even after the Hyksos were defeated. Ahmose also had to deal with Kush to the south. He campaigned in Nubia, reasserting Egyptian control over territories that had been lost during the Second Intermediate Period. He had to suppress rebellions within Egypt itself as well; there are references to uprisings that he had to crush, suggesting not everyone was enthusiastic about Theban rule.

By the end of Ahmose's reign around 1525 BCE, Egypt was reunified under a single ruler for the first time in over two hundred years. The Second Intermediate Period was over, and the New Kingdom had begun.

Building an Empire

The New Kingdom would be fundamentally different from the Middle Kingdom that had preceded it. The experience of fighting the Hyksos, combined with new military technologies, evolving ideology, economic opportunities, and institutional changes, had transformed Egyptian attitudes about the outside world and militarized Egyptian society. During the Old and Middle Kingdoms, Egypt had generally been content to defend its borders and conduct limited military operations to secure resources. Egypt saw itself as the center of civilization; there was no need to expand beyond its natural borders.

The Hyksos occupation shattered this complacency. Egyptians learned that even their seemingly impregnable homeland could be penetrated and occupied by foreigners. The lesson they took from this was that defense wasn't enough. Egypt needed to project power beyond its borders, create buffer zones of controlled or dominated territories, and ensure that foreign threats never again reached Egyptian soil.

The military that made this expansion possible had been transformed during the struggle against the Hyksos. Egypt now maintained professional military forces made of career soldiers who trained regularly and campaigned frequently. They were supplemented by conscripts and foreign mercenaries, particularly Nubians who were valued as warriors. This was a significant shift from the Egyptians' earlier reliance on laborers.

Most importantly, chariots became the elite striking force of the Egyptian army. Egyptian charioteers, drawn from the nobility, trained extensively in the skills required to fight from a moving chariot. They learned how to drive, shoot composite bows, and coordinate with other chariots. Egyptian chariots were lighter and faster than those used by most other Near Eastern armies, giving Egypt a tactical advantage.

The composite bow, made from wood, horn, and sinew, was far more powerful than the simple bows Egyptians had used previously. It could penetrate armor at greater range, making Egyptian archers devastating on the battlefield. Combined with chariots, which provided mobility and allowed archers to shoot while moving, this created a formidable military force.

The Egyptian military also developed sophisticated logistics and organizational systems. Campaigning in Syria meant marching hundreds of miles from Egypt, supplying armies in foreign territory, maintaining siege equipment, and coordinating operations across vast distances. Egyptian scribes kept detailed records of military organization, supply requirements, and campaign plans. This allowed Egypt to project power far beyond its borders in ways that would have been impossible during earlier periods.

This aggressive, expansionist mentality defined the New Kingdom. Ahmose I had reunified Egypt, but his immediate successors would take the next step. They would expand Egyptian power, creating an empire that would make Egypt the superpower of the ancient Near East.

This expansion began in earnest with Thutmose I (approximately 1504-1492 BCE), the third pharaoh of the Eighteenth Dynasty. Thutmose I campaigned vigorously in both directions. He moved south into Nubia and north into the Levant and Syria. Royal inscriptions credit him with pushing Egyptian control far to the south in Nubia, beyond the Third Cataract of the Nile, and deeper into Sudan than the Middle Kingdom had ever controlled, though the full scope of this control remains debated among scholars. He erected a boundary stela near the Third Cataract, marking the claimed southern extent of Egyptian power. Nubia wasn't just conquered; it was annexed, becoming an Egyptian province administered by an Egyptian official called the "King's Son of Kush" (he usually wasn't actually the king's son—it was an administrative title).

But why was Nubia so important? The same reason it always had been: gold. Nubia was rich in gold deposits, and the New Kingdom pharaohs ruthlessly exploited them. Nubian gold financed Egypt's armies, building projects, and diplomatic efforts. The wealth flowing from Nubia helped make Egypt's imperial expansion possible.

Thutmose I's campaigns in Syria–Palestine (the Levant) were even more significant. According to royal inscriptions, he marched an Egyptian army through Palestine, into Syria, all the way to the Euphrates River. This was farther north than any Egyptian army had gone before. He reportedly erected a victory stela on the banks of the Euphrates, marking what he probably saw as the northern limit of the civilized world.

The Levant was a complex political landscape, dotted with city-states—small kingdoms centered on fortified cities, each with its own ruler. These city-states were wealthy from agriculture and trade, but they were also vulnerable. They constantly competed with each other and were threatened by larger powers. Egyptian conquest offered both threat and opportunity. Submit to Egypt, pay tribute, and you received Egyptian protection and trade access. Resist, and you faced the Egyptian military force.

Thutmose I's campaigns established the pattern that would define Egyptian imperialism for the next several centuries. Egypt didn't directly annex and administer most of the Levant the way it did with Nubia. Instead, it created a system of vassal states. Local rulers remained in power, governing their own territories, but they acknowledged Egyptian suzerainty, paid tribute, and were expected to support Egyptian military operations. Egyptian officials and small garrisons were stationed at key locations to monitor the vassals and intervene if necessary.

This system was relatively efficient from Egypt's perspective. It gave the Egyptians tribute, resources, and security without the full costs of direct administration and occupation. But it also required constant maintenance. Vassal rulers might rebel or stop paying tribute if they thought they could get away with it. Rival powers—particularly Mitanni to the north and later the Hittites—would try to lure Egyptian vassals into their own spheres of influence. Egyptian pharaohs had to be prepared to campaign regularly in the Levant to maintain their dominance.

The wealth flowing into Egypt from its expanding empire was enormous. Tribute came from Nubia, the Levantine vassals, defeated enemies, and trade. This wealth funded massive building projects at home, supported an expanded bureaucracy, enriched the temples (particularly the Temple of Amun at Karnak, which became fantastically wealthy), and created a golden age of prosperity.

The empire also brought cultural exchange. Egyptian art and culture spread throughout the empire, influencing vassal states. Egypt also absorbed influences from its empire, such as foreign goods, foreign artistic motifs, foreign gods, and foreign peoples (prisoners of war, slaves, traders, and diplomats). The New Kingdom would be more cosmopolitan and more internationally engaged than any previous period of Egyptian history.

However, having a large empire brought challenges. As mentioned, managing vassal states required constant attention. Military campaigns were expensive and dangerous. Egyptian sons died fighting in Syria or Nubia. The wealth and power concentrated in the hands of the military elite and the priesthood of Amun could create challenges to royal authority. Egypt also faced rivals who could threaten its empire, particularly Mitanni, a powerful kingdom in northern Syria, which would compete with Egypt for control of the Levant throughout the 15th century BCE.

The Pharaoh Queen

In the midst of this aggressive, militaristic New Kingdom, one of ancient Egypt's most remarkable rulers came to power: Hatshepsut (approximately 1479–1458 BCE), a woman who declared herself pharaoh and ruled Egypt for over two decades.

Hatshepsut's rise to power was unusual, but it was not entirely unprecedented in the complicated world of Egyptian royal succession. She was the daughter of Thutmose I and his principal wife, Ahmose. When Thutmose I died, the throne passed to Thutmose II, who was probably Hatshepsut's half-brother (royal incest was common in New Kingdom Egypt as a way to keep power within the royal family). Hatshepsut married Thutmose II, making her both his half-sister and his wife. She became queen.

Thutmose II's reign was relatively brief and apparently not particularly distinguished. When he died around 1479 BCE, the succession situation was complicated. The designated heir was Thutmose III, a young boy, the son of Thutmose II by a secondary wife named Iset. Thutmose III was legitimate, but he was very young. He was probably only around two to four years old.

In such situations, it was normal for a regent to govern until the young king came of age. Hatshepsut, as the young king's stepmother and the daughter and wife of pharaohs, was the obvious choice for regent. So far, this was all conventional.

What happened next was not. Within a few years of becoming regent, Hatshepsut declared herself pharaoh—not queen regent, not queen consort, but pharaoh, with all the titles, regalia, and authority of a male king. She adopted the full royal titulary, including the names and titles reserved for pharaohs. She wore the traditional pharaonic regalia, including the false beard that symbolized kingship. In artistic representations, she was often depicted with a male body, wearing the traditional king's kilt, though sometimes with feminine features or in some cases clearly as a woman in the king's regalia.

A statue of Hatshepsut.[13]

Why did Hatshepsut take this unprecedented step? The sources don't tell us directly, but we can speculate. Perhaps she believed she was the most qualified person to rule. She was, after all, of the direct royal bloodline and the daughter and wife of kings, while Thutmose III was the son of a secondary wife. Perhaps she had ambitions to rule in her own right, not just as a regent for someone else. Perhaps she saw political challenges that required a pharaoh's full authority to address. Or perhaps it was simply that she could—she had the power, the support, and the will to make it happen.

Hatshepsut's justification for her rule was clever. She claimed that the god Amun himself had decreed she should be king. Elaborate texts and reliefs at her mortuary temple at Deir el-Bahri describe how Amun took the form of Thutmose I and impregnated Ahmose with a divine child—Hatshepsut herself. This "divine birth" narrative, borrowed from traditional royal ideology, presented Hatshepsut as not just legitimate but chosen by the gods.

She also emphasized her royal lineage, presenting herself as Thutmose I's intended heir, the only legitimate child of his principal wife. In her narrative, her rule was the natural continuation of her father's reign, which had been briefly interrupted by the relatively unimportant reign of Thutmose II.

What's remarkable is that Hatshepsut's claim to kingship seems to have been largely accepted. There's no evidence of civil war or significant opposition. The key officials of the kingdom, including Senenmut, her chief steward and probably closest advisor, and other high officials, supported her rule. Thutmose III, the young king she had displaced, remained alive and held some royal status, but he was clearly subordinate. How he felt about this arrangement we can only guess, but he was in no position to challenge Hatshepsut during her lifetime.

Hatshepsut's reign was notable for its focus on building projects and trade expeditions rather than military conquest. This doesn't mean she neglected military affairs—there's evidence of some military campaigns during her reign, particularly in Nubia—but her reign wasn't characterized by the aggressive expansionism of her predecessor and successor.

Her most famous achievement was the trading expedition to Punt, the legendary land far to the south (probably somewhere on the Red Sea coast of modern Sudan, Eritrea, or Somalia). The expedition is commemorated in elaborate reliefs at her mortuary temple, showing ships being loaded with exotic goods like myrrh trees, incense, ebony, ivory, gold, and exotic animals, including baboons. The reliefs even depict the ruler of Punt and his obese wife, a rare example of Egyptian artists depicting foreign rulers with individualized features rather than generic types.

A drawing of the relief of the expedition to Punt.[18]

The Punt expedition wasn't just about acquiring exotic goods; it was also about prestige and demonstrating royal power. A pharaoh who could organize expeditions to distant lands, bring back fabulous wealth, and present incense to the gods was demonstrating the same power and divine favor that earlier pharaohs had shown through military conquest.

Hatshepsut's greatest legacy is in architecture. Her mortuary temple at Deir el-Bahri, on the west bank of the Nile at Thebes, is one of ancient Egypt's most beautiful buildings. Designed by Senenmut, it consists of three terraced colonnades built against the cliff face. The temple's reliefs tell the story of Hatshepsut's reign, including the Punt expedition, her divine birth, her building projects, and her offerings to the gods.

Hatshepsut's mortuary temple at Deir el-Bahri.[14]

She also built extensively at Karnak Temple, adding obelisks, pylons (gateways), and other structures to Amun's great temple complex. These building projects enriched the priesthood of Amun and demonstrated royal piety, reinforcing the connection between the pharaoh and the gods.

Hatshepsut ruled for approximately twenty-two years, dying around 1458 BCE. The circumstances of her death are unknown. We don't know if she died of natural causes, was overthrown, or was assassinated. What we do know is that after her death, Thutmose III, after spending decades as junior partner to his stepmother, took full control of Egypt.

Late in his reign—probably at least twenty years after Hatshepsut's death—Thutmose III ordered Hatshepsut's names and images to be systematically removed from monuments throughout Egypt. Her cartouches (an oval frame with the name of an Egyptian ruler inside) were chiseled out. Her statues were smashed or buried. Her name was erased from the king lists. This was *damnatio memoriae*—the erasure of someone from history.

Why did Thutmose III wait so long to do this? And why did he do it at all? These questions have generated much scholarly debate. Some argue it was personal resentment, a form of revenge for being kept from power for so long. Others suggest it was political. Perhaps late in his reign, Thutmose III faced succession challenges and wanted to ensure his own line succeeded by erasing the precedent of a female pharaoh. Others suggest it was ideological. The concept of a female pharaoh violated ma'at, the proper order, and needed to be erased.

Whatever the reason, Thutmose III's erasure campaign was largely successful. For thousands of years, Hatshepsut was almost completely forgotten, her monuments attributed to other pharaohs. Only in the 19th and 20th centuries did modern archaeologists and historians piece together her story, recognizing her as one of ancient Egypt's most successful and remarkable rulers.

Hatshepsut's reign demonstrated that a woman could successfully exercise power, manage the bureaucracy, conduct foreign policy, and maintain Egypt's position. However, the erasure of her memory also showed the limits of that achievement. Egyptian ideology was fundamentally patriarchal, and a female pharaoh represented a disruption of the proper order that needed to be corrected, even retrospectively.

After Hatshepsut, Egypt would return to aggressive military expansion under Thutmose III, who proved to be one of ancient Egypt's greatest conquerors.

Chapter 8:
Warriors and Conquerors

Thutmose III: The Napoleon of Ancient Egypt

After Hatshepsut's death around 1458 BCE, Thutmose III finally became the sole ruler of Egypt. He had been king in name for many years—sources suggest over twenty years, though this is partly inferred from incomplete records—but he had always been subordinate to his stepmother. Now, approaching middle age, he was finally free to rule on his own terms. And what he chose to do with that freedom would make him one of ancient Egypt's greatest military leaders.

Thutmose III (approximately 1479-1425 BCE, though effectively sole ruler only from around 1458 BCE) conducted numerous military campaigns during his reign—sources suggest

Thutmose III.[15]

at least seventeen, though the exact count and dating are debated among scholars—most of them in Syria-Palestine. He would push Egyptian control farther north than any pharaoh before him, defeat powerful coalitions of enemies, and establish Egyptian dominance over the Levant so thoroughly that it would last for generations. Later historians would compare him to Napoleon Bonaparte. Both were relatively short men (Thutmose's mummy suggests he was about 5'3" tall) who became military geniuses, conducting numerous campaigns, winning decisive battles, and building empires through aggressive warfare, though Thutmose's empire lasted much longer than Napoleon's did.

The first and most famous of Thutmose III's campaigns came early in his sole reign: the Battle of Megiddo in approximately 1457 BCE. This battle would become the most documented military engagement from ancient Egypt, described in detail in inscriptions at Karnak Temple.

A coalition of Canaanite and Syrian city-states, led by the ruler of Kadesh and possibly supported by the kingdom of Mitanni far to the north, had rebelled against Egyptian authority. They assembled their forces at the fortified city of Megiddo, strategically located in northern Palestine and controlling important trade routes. This was a serious challenge to Egyptian dominance in the region, and if successful, could have unraveled Egyptian control throughout Syria-Palestine.

Thutmose III responded with a major military expedition. He marched his army from Egypt through Palestine toward Megiddo. When he reached the vicinity of the city, he faced a strategic choice. There were three possible routes through the Carmel mountain ridge to reach Megiddo: a southern route and a northern route. They were both relatively safe but indirect. A central route through a narrow mountain pass would bring his army out directly in front of Megiddo, but it was potentially dangerous.

His generals advised taking one of the safer routes. However, Thutmose III chose the risky central route, reasoning that the enemy would expect him to take a safer path and would position their forces accordingly. It was a gamble. If the enemy caught his army strung out in the narrow pass, they could be destroyed. But Thutmose was right. His army emerged from the pass to find the enemy unprepared, their forces divided and not positioned to defend against an attack from that direction.

The battle was fought on the plain before Megiddo. The Egyptian inscriptions describe it in detail: the positioning of the forces, Thutmose

III fighting from his chariot, the enemy formation breaking and fleeing into the fortified city. The Egyptians pursued, but they couldn't capture the city immediately. The defenders closed the gates, and some soldiers had to be hauled up the walls with ropes and sheets lowered by the people inside.

According to the Egyptian inscriptions, the Egyptians built a fortification wall around the entire city to prevent escape or resupply. The siege of Megiddo lasted approximately seven months before the city finally surrendered. While these details come from Egyptian triumphal accounts—and the lengthy siege has been questioned by some modern scholars as possibly exaggerated—the scale of the victory is clear. Thutmose III captured enormous plunder, including horses, chariots, gold, silver, weapons, armor, and livestock. More importantly, he captured or received the submission of the rulers of numerous city-states that had been part of the rebellion.

The victory at Megiddo was decisive. It broke the coalition against Egypt, reasserted Egyptian dominance in Palestine, and showed that rebellion against Egyptian authority would be met with swift and overwhelming force. And this was only the beginning of Thutmose III's military career.

Over the next two decades, Thutmose III campaigned almost annually in Syria-Palestine. Each campaign had specific objectives. He wanted to punish rebellious vassal states, collect tribute from submissive ones, capture strategic cities, intimidate potential rivals, and gradually extend Egyptian control farther north. Some campaigns were major military expeditions involving battles and sieges. Others were more like royal marches through Egyptian-controlled territory, where the pharaoh's presence reinforced Egyptian authority and vassal rulers came to present tribute and renew their oaths of loyalty.

Thutmose III pushed Egyptian power to its greatest extent. He campaigned as far north as the Euphrates River, which was even farther than his grandfather Thutmose I had gone. He crossed the Euphrates—a feat requiring boats to be built or transported overland—and erected a victory stela on the far bank, next to the stela his grandfather had placed there decades earlier. Egyptian influence extended, at least nominally, from the Fourth Cataract of the Nile in Nubia to the Euphrates in Syria, a distance of over 1,500 miles.

However, maintaining this empire required constant effort. The Levantine city-states were constantly shifting in their loyalties. Local rulers had their own ambitions and would rebel if they thought Egyptian attention was elsewhere. The kingdom of Mitanni to the north was a powerful rival that constantly worked to undermine Egyptian influence and bring Syrian states into its own sphere of influence. This far-flung system required frequent campaigns, and Egyptian influence in distant regions could weaken or collapse quickly when the pharaoh's attention waned.

Thutmose III's solution was a system combining military force, political management, and ideological control. Military force came from regular campaigns; showing up with an army reminded vassals that rebellion had consequences. Political management involved carefully handling the local rulers. Some were left in place if they were loyal, and others were replaced with pro-Egyptian rulers. Sons of local rulers were sometimes taken to Egypt as hostages (or guests, depending on your perspective), where they would be educated in Egyptian ways before being sent back to rule their homelands. Ideological control involved promoting the idea that the Egyptian pharaoh was the supreme ruler ordained by the gods and that serving Egypt brought prosperity while rebelling brought destruction.

The wealth flowing into Egypt from this empire was staggering. The Karnak inscriptions list tribute from Thutmose III's campaigns: gold, silver, copper, lapis lazuli, exotic wood, incense, oil, wine, cattle, horses, chariots, prisoners, and slaves. This wealth enriched the royal treasury, supported the army, funded massive building projects, and benefited the Temple of Amun at Karnak, which received substantial donations from the king and grew incredibly wealthy and powerful.

Thutmose III was also a prolific builder. He constructed extensively at Karnak, adding halls, obelisks, and monuments. His mortuary temple at Thebes (now mostly destroyed) was a major structure. He left inscriptions throughout Egypt and the conquered territories, proclaiming his victories and his devotion to the gods.

When Thutmose III died around 1425 BCE after approximately fifty-four years as king (thirty-two as sole ruler), he left Egypt at the height of its power. The empire was secure, the treasury was full, the military was battle-tested and confident, and Egyptian prestige was at its highest point. His son Amenhotep II would inherit a stable, powerful empire—the fruits of decades of military campaigning and administrative development.

Thutmose III deserves his reputation as one of ancient Egypt's greatest pharaohs. He was a skilled military commander who understood strategy and tactics, a capable administrator who managed a vast empire, and a ruler who combined military force with political intelligence.

The Riches of Empire

The decades following Thutmose III's death saw Egypt at perhaps its wealthiest and most powerful. His son, Amenhotep II (approximately 1427–1400 BCE), and grandson, Thutmose IV (approximately 1400–1390 BCE), maintained the empire, conducting occasional military campaigns but mostly benefiting from the system Thutmose III had established. However, it was Amenhotep III (approximately 1390–1352 BCE), Thutmose IV's son, whose reign represented the absolute peak of New Kingdom wealth, power, and artistic achievement.

Amenhotep III ruled for thirty-eight years over an Egypt that was secure, prosperous, and culturally sophisticated. His reign was largely peaceful. He conducted minimal military campaigns, with perhaps one known major expedition in Nubia during his fifth year. For most of his reign, Egypt was at peace. This wasn't because threats had disappeared but because the empire was so stable and Egyptian dominance so complete that major military expeditions weren't necessary. The system of vassal states functioned smoothly, tribute flowed regularly into Egypt, and potential rivals were either intimidated by Egyptian power or preoccupied with their own problems.

The wealth accumulated from decades of empire was now available for the king to spend on building, arts, and luxury on an unprecedented scale, and spend it he did. Amenhotep III's building program was massive. At Thebes, he constructed a mortuary temple on the west bank that was among the largest religious structures built in Egypt. Reconstructions based on surviving evidence suggest it was over seven hundred feet long and five hundred feet wide. Almost nothing of it survives today except for two massive statues of the king that once flanked the entrance. These statues, known as the Colossi of Memnon, are over sixty feet tall.

Amenhotep III's mortuary temple in 2014. Those two tall statues in the center are the Colossi.[16]

At Luxor, Amenhotep III built most of what is now Luxor Temple, a beautiful structure dedicated to Amun. At Karnak, he added structures including a huge pylon (gateway) and numerous statues. He built palaces, including a sprawling palace complex at Malkata on the west bank of Thebes that served as his primary residence. He constructed temples throughout Egypt and in Nubia. Everywhere he built, he built large, richly decorated structures with the finest materials (granite, sandstone, costly imported wood, and gold).

The artistic quality of work from Amenhotep III's reign was exceptional. Egyptian artists had centuries of tradition to draw on, but during his reign, they achieved a level of elegance that many consider the high point of Egyptian art. Statues show remarkable naturalism within Egyptian artistic conventions. The famous seated statues of Amenhotep III show the king as mature and dignified, with subtle modeling and refined proportions. Reliefs are carved with exquisite delicacy. Painting achieves subtle gradations of color.

Private tombs from this period—tombs of nobles and officials—show similar high quality. Tomb paintings depict banquet scenes, hunting, religious rituals, and daily life, with both technical skill and artistic imagination. These tombs give us our most detailed views of elite life in ancient Egypt, showing clothing, furniture, food, entertainment, and social interaction.

Amenhotep III's court was lavish and cosmopolitan. Foreign ambassadors came to Egypt from throughout the Near East, from the Hittites in Anatolia, to the Mitanni in Syria, to the Babylonians in Mesopotamia. They brought gifts and sought Egyptian favor. The Amarna Letters—diplomatic correspondence from slightly later in the New Kingdom—give us a glimpse of this diplomatic world. Foreign rulers addressed the Egyptian pharaoh as "brother," though with the understanding that Egypt was first among equals. They sent tribute and requested Egyptian gold, which Egypt possessed in abundance from Nubian mines.

The wealth of Amenhotep III's court is evident in the gifts he gave. He sent gold statues, furniture overlaid with gold, jewelry, and luxury goods to foreign rulers. He commissioned hundreds of large stone sculptures for temples. He created a large number of scarabs (seal amulets) commemorating various events of his reign. These commemorative scarabs were distributed widely, serving both as royal propaganda and as gifts that demonstrated the king's wealth.

A scarab commemorating Amenhotep III's marriage to one of his wives."

Amenhotep III married many women, as polygamy was standard for pharaohs, but his principal wife was Tiye. She played an unusually prominent role. Tiye was depicted alongside the king in official art more than most queens. She was mentioned in diplomatic correspondence and seems to have wielded real influence. After Amenhotep III's death, she remained influential during their son's reign. Tiye wasn't of royal blood herself—her father is believed to have been a chariot officer and her mother a palace lady-in-waiting—but she rose to become one of ancient Egypt's most powerful queens.

His reign also saw interesting religious developments. While Amenhotep III maintained traditional religious practices and built temples to the traditional gods, there is evidence of growing emphasis on solar deities, particularly the sun disk called the Aten. Some scholars see this as foreshadowing the religious revolution that would take over Egypt during the next reign, though Amenhotep III remained orthodox in his public religious observances.

The king celebrated at least three Sed festivals, traditional jubilee celebrations of royal power that were supposed to occur after thirty years of rule but could be celebrated more frequently. They included the symbolic rejuvenation of the king, religious ceremonies throughout Egypt, and the massive distribution of gifts. The Sed festivals served both religious and political purposes. They demonstrated royal vitality, redistributed wealth, and reinforced the king's relationship with the gods and with his subjects.

Toward the end of his reign, Amenhotep III became ill. Exactly what afflicted him is unclear. His mummy shows signs of various health problems, including severe dental disease and what some scholars interpret as possible obesity, though this is debated due to potential embalming distortion. He might have suffered from painful conditions that made his final years difficult. However, he continued ruling until his death around 1352 BCE; it was one of the longest and most prosperous reigns in Egyptian history.

Amenhotep III's reign represents the high point of New Kingdom Egypt in many ways. The empire was at its most stable. Wealth was at its peak. Art and architecture reached their highest achievements. Egypt dominated the ancient Near East without needing to fight constant wars to maintain that dominance.

But this golden age contained the seeds of crisis. The massive wealth flowing to the Temple of Amun had made the priesthood extremely powerful, potentially rivaling even royal authority. The diplomatic balance that kept peace with Egypt's rivals was delicate and would eventually break down. And the royal succession would bring to the throne one of ancient Egypt's most controversial rulers. His radical religious reforms would nearly tear the Egyptian state apart.

For now, though, Egypt basked in the glory of Amenhotep III's reign. It was Egypt's golden age, and those who lived through it probably believed it would last forever. However, dramatic changes were coming, and they would begin with Amenhotep III's son and successor, who would call himself Akhenaten.

Chapter 9: The Heretic Pharaoh — Akhenaten's Revolution

One God, One City, One Vision

When Amenhotep IV came to the throne around 1352 BCE, nobody could have predicted what was coming. He was the son of Amenhotep III and Queen Tiye, and he inherited an empire at its peak. By all expectations, he would continue his father's policies, maintain the traditional religious practices, conduct the necessary military campaigns to keep vassals in line, and build monuments to the gods while living in luxury. That's what pharaohs did.

Instead, Amenhotep IV would launch the most radical religious revolution in ancient Egyptian history. He would abandon the traditional gods that Egyptians had worshiped for millennia. He would change his own name, build a completely new capital city, and move the entire government there. He would transform Egyptian art into something unrecognizable. And his reforms would severely destabilize the Egyptian state, weakening it both internally and in its international standing.

Early in his reign, Amenhotep IV seemed conventional enough. He was crowned at Thebes, the traditional capital. He married Nefertiti, who would become one of ancient Egypt's most famous queens. He began building projects at Karnak, the great Temple of Amun. Everything appeared normal.

Statue of Akhenaten.[18]

But there were hints of what was coming. The early building projects showed increased emphasis on the sun disk, the Aten. This wasn't entirely unprecedented. Sun worship had always been important in Egypt, and his father, Amenhotep III, had shown interest in solar deities. However, Amenhotep IV took this much further.

By around his fifth year on the throne, the changes accelerated dramatically. Amenhotep IV declared that the Aten was the supreme god. Whether this was true monotheism (the worship of only one god), monolatry (the worship of one god while acknowledging others exist), or henotheism (one supreme god above others) remains debated among scholars. What's clear is that Amenhotep IV rejected the worship of traditional gods and focused his devotion exclusively on the Aten. This was a dramatic break with Egyptian polytheistic tradition that had existed for millennia.

To emphasize this break with tradition, Amenhotep IV changed his name. "Amenhotep" meant "Amun is satisfied," a name that honored the god Amun, whom Amenhotep IV now declared was false. He took a new name, Akhenaten, meaning "effective for the Aten" or "servant of the Aten." From this point on, we'll call him Akhenaten, the name by which he's remembered.

Akhenaten didn't stop with religious reform. He decided to build an entirely new capital city. He couldn't stay in Thebes. That was Amun's city, dominated by the priesthood of Amun and filled with temples to the traditional gods. He needed a clean break, a city devoted solely to the Aten.

Akhenaten chose a site in Middle Egypt that had never been occupied before—a stretch of desert on the east bank of the Nile backed by imposing cliffs. The cliffs formed a natural bay framing the rising sun, creating powerful imagery for a sun-worshiping cult, and the site allowed him to build without associating with traditional religious centers. He named it Akhetaten, "Horizon of the Aten" (modern scholars call the site Amarna). He marked the city's boundaries with a series of stone stelae carved into the cliffs, in which he swore never to move beyond these boundaries, binding both himself and his successors to this site forever.

The construction of Akhetaten began around year five or six of Akhenaten's reign and proceeded with remarkable speed. Within a few years, an entire city had risen from the desert. There were palaces, temples, administrative buildings, workshops, residential neighborhoods, and tombs cut into the cliffs. By year eight or nine, Akhenaten, Nefertiti, their six daughters, and the royal court had relocated to Akhetaten. The government moved. The bureaucracy moved. Elite families built houses there. Akhetaten became Egypt's capital. Thebes, Memphis, and the other traditional cities were abandoned by the royal family and the highest levels of government.

The Great Temple of the Aten at Akhetaten emphasized openness and light, representing a significant departure from traditional Egyptian temples. Traditional temples were dark, mysterious places with enclosed sanctuaries where cult statues of gods resided in dim chambers. Only priests could enter the inner sanctuaries.

The Great Temple of the Aten featured large open courtyards exposed to the sky, with hundreds of altars spread across them. While some traditional temple features remained and archaeological evidence indicates architectural variation within Amarna, the emphasis was clearly on worshiping in sunlight rather than enclosed darkness. Worship of the Aten meant worshiping the sun itself, and that worship happened in full daylight, under the sun's rays. The temple was oriented so the sun would rise directly along its axis, flooding it with light at dawn.

Akhenaten positioned himself as the sole intermediary between the Aten and humanity. In the traditional Egyptian religion, many priests could serve the gods, and laypeople could worship at temples and shrines. In Atenism (as modern scholars call Akhenaten's religion), only Akhenaten could truly worship the Aten, and only through Akhenaten could people access the divine. This made the pharaoh even more central to religious life than before, but it also meant that if you wanted to worship the Aten, you had to go through Akhenaten.

Nefertiti played an unusually prominent role in this religious system. She was depicted in religious scenes alongside Akhenaten, both of them worshiping the Aten and receiving the sun's rays. She appears to have been an active participant in religious rituals, as she was depicted in ways that suggest she had significant religious and possibly political authority, though the full extent of her power remains a subject of scholarly debate. Some reliefs show her in poses and contexts that were typically royal privileges. This level of prominence for a queen was unprecedented in Egyptian royal ideology.

Why did Akhenaten do all of this? What motivated such radical changes? These are questions that have fascinated and frustrated scholars for over a century, and there's no consensus answer.

Some scholars see it as a genuine religious conviction. Perhaps Akhenaten truly believed that the Aten was the only god and that he had a divine mission to convert Egypt to this truth. The hymns to the Aten—particularly the Great Hymn to the Aten, which might have been composed by Akhenaten himself—show real poetic beauty and theological complexity. They describe the Aten as the creator of all life, the source of all light and warmth, and the sustainer of the world. There's a universalism in Atenism that differs from traditional Egyptian religion. The Aten creates and sustains all lands and all peoples, not just Egypt. This could reflect genuine philosophical and theological thinking.

Others see political motivation. The priesthood of Amun at Thebes had become enormously wealthy and powerful. By rejecting Amun and the other traditional gods, Akhenaten broke the power of the old priesthoods. He confiscated their lands and wealth, shut down their temples, and created a new religious system where he was unchallenged as the sole religious authority. From this perspective, Atenism was a power grab disguised as religious reform.

Still others see psychological factors. Some scholars have suggested Akhenaten had physical or mental health issues that affected his behavior. Artistic depictions show him with an unusual body shape. Some medical experts have suggested various conditions, though diagnosing ancient diseases from artistic representations is highly speculative.

Most likely, multiple factors were involved. Akhenaten might have been genuinely religious while also recognizing the political advantages of breaking the old priesthoods. He might have had personal reasons for rejecting the traditional religion while also pursuing his own goals of centralizing power. People are complex, and their motivations often are too.

Modern scholarly interpretations of Akhenaten have varied widely. Early scholars, influenced by their own religious backgrounds, saw him as a proto-monotheist, a visionary who preceded Judaism and Christianity by worshiping one god. Sigmund Freud even wrote a book arguing that Moses was an Egyptian priest who learned monotheism from Akhenaten. This theory is almost universally rejected by scholars, but it shows how fascinated people were by the idea of ancient monotheism. Later scholars took more critical views. Some saw Akhenaten as a failed tyrant who nearly destroyed Egypt by pursuing his obsessions. Others viewed him as mentally ill or physically disabled. More recent scholarship has tried to understand him in his own context, examining the political, religious, and social factors that might have motivated his reforms.

What's clear is that Akhenaten didn't just stop worshiping the old gods himself; he attempted to suppress the traditional religion throughout Egypt. State temples to the traditional gods were closed. Their priesthoods were disbanded. Most dramatically, Akhenaten ordered the names of the old gods, particularly Amun, erased from monuments throughout Egypt. Workers went from temple to tomb, chiseling out the names wherever they appeared. Even his father's name, Amenhotep, was targeted because it contained "Amun."

This was spiritual warfare. By erasing the gods' names, Akhenaten was trying to erase their existence. In Egyptian belief, names had power. To speak a name was to make something real. By removing these names, Akhenaten was attempting to unmake the old gods and render them non-existent.

For devout Egyptians who had worshiped these gods their entire lives, who had been taught that Osiris judged the dead and that Isis protected children and that Horus was the divine king, this must have been profoundly disturbing. Their entire religious worldview was being overturned by royal decree. The gods their ancestors had worshiped for thousands of years were declared false. The temples where they had prayed were closed. The festivals that had marked the rhythm of their year were cancelled.

However, this state-mandated suppression was complex and uneven across Egypt. While the official cults were dismantled, archaeological evidence suggests that household worship of traditional gods continued in private, showing the limits of the revolution's reach into everyday religious life. Evidence from elsewhere in Egypt suggests that many people continued traditional practices in private, keeping small shrines to the old gods in their homes, hidden from official scrutiny. Even at Amarna itself, amulets of Bes (the god who protected households and children), Taweret (the goddess of childbirth), and other household gods have been found. People apparently went through the motions of Aten worship publicly while maintaining traditional practices privately.

Art, Life, and the Weakening Empire

The religious revolution wasn't the only radical change Akhenaten instituted. He also transformed Egyptian art in ways that were just as dramatic and far more visible.

Traditional Egyptian art had been remarkably consistent for over a thousand years. It followed strict conventions: figures shown in profile with the eye viewed from the front, bodies idealized and eternally youthful, and formal compositions emphasizing order and hierarchy. Royal statues showed kings as ageless and perfect, embodying divine power. This style had varied somewhat over time, but the basic conventions remained the same.

Akhenaten's art was radically different. Early in his reign, a new artistic style appeared, the Amarna style. It showed the royal family in ways that broke nearly every convention of traditional Egyptian art.

Akhenaten was depicted with an extremely unusual body. He had an elongated head, a long, thin neck, narrow shoulders, a prominent belly, wide hips, and spindly arms and legs. His face was shown with a long jaw, thick lips, and heavy-lidded eyes. These features were so extreme that early scholars thought they must represent some physical deformity or disease. More recent scholarship suggests it was deliberate stylization. Akhenaten chose to be represented this way.

Nefertiti was shown in this same style, with an elongated skull and distinctive features. Their six daughters were also depicted with the same elongated skulls and unusual proportions. Even courtiers and officials adopted this style in their own depictions.

A relief depicting Akhenaten (his head is lost), Nefertiti, and one of their daughters.[19]

Why? Several theories exist. Some scholars suggest the style was meant to convey religious meaning. Perhaps it was meant to show the royal family as neither fully male nor fully female, transcending normal human categories and purely existing as intermediaries between the divine and the earthly. Others suggest it was meant to emphasize the royal family's divine nature by showing them as different from ordinary humans. Still others think it simply reflected Akhenaten's personal aesthetic preferences or even that he genuinely looked unusual and chose to have everyone depicted in his image.

Whatever the reason, the style was unlike anything in Egyptian art before or after. It appeared suddenly at the start of Akhenaten's reign and disappeared just as suddenly after his death, suggesting it was specifically tied to his rule.

However, the Amarna style wasn't just about unusual body proportions. It also showed unprecedented intimacy and informality in royal imagery. Traditional Egyptian royal art showed pharaohs as distant, formal figures performing religious rituals or smiting enemies. Amarna art showed Akhenaten and Nefertiti in domestic scenes, playing with their daughters, embracing each other, sitting casually, and even kissing. The royal family was shown as a family, with affection and informal interaction.

One famous relief shows Akhenaten and Nefertiti sitting together, their small daughters climbing on them, playing. The sun's rays shine down on them, each ray ending in a little hand, blessing the family. It's charming and completely unlike the formal, distant royal imagery that had dominated Egyptian art for centuries.

Akhenaten, Nefertiti, and their children.[20]

Was this informality genuine? Did Akhenaten and Nefertiti really have an affectionate family life? Or was this political propaganda, presenting the royal family as the perfect family blessed by the Aten? We can't know for sure, but the images are striking.

Life at Amarna was also unusual. The city was built quickly, mostly in mudbrick rather than stone. It was designed to serve as the capital, but it did not have the centuries of accumulated grandeur that places like Thebes or Memphis had. The city stretched along the east bank of the Nile for several miles and was organized into districts.

The central city contained the official buildings: the Great Palace, the Great Temple of the Aten, administrative offices, and military quarters. The royal family lived in the North Palace, which was separated from the main city. Elite officials built large houses in the northern suburb and elsewhere. Ordinary workers lived in a purpose-built workers' village to the south.

The elite houses at Amarna show interesting features. They were large, often over thirty rooms, and organized around central courtyards. They had gardens, chapels, storage magazines, and servant quarters. The houses show clear social stratification. Elite officials lived in comfort, with space and amenities. But even these grand houses were built quickly in mudbrick, without the stone construction that would make them permanent.

The site has been extensively excavated, and it has provided unusually detailed information about daily life in ancient Egypt. Archaeologists have found everything from grand palaces to workers' houses, from royal correspondence to household waste. The Amarna Letters—diplomatic correspondence written on clay tablets in Akkadian (the diplomatic language of the time)—were discovered here, providing invaluable information about international relations during this period.

These letters reveal problems that were developing during Akhenaten's reign. Foreign rulers wrote to the pharaoh complaining about the lack of Egyptian support. Vassal rulers in Syria-Palestine reported attacks from neighboring states or from groups like the Hapiru (possibly related to the Hebrews, though this connection is debated) and begged for Egyptian military assistance. The letters suggest Egyptian control over its empire was weakening.

Akhenaten seems to have neglected foreign policy and military affairs. There's no evidence he ever conducted a military campaign. He didn't campaign in Syria–Palestine to maintain control over vassals, and he didn't lead expeditions to Nubia. He might have been so focused on his religious revolution and on building Amarna that he neglected the practical business of maintaining the empire his ancestors had built.

The consequences were serious. Egyptian influence in Syria–Palestine declined. Vassal states stopped sending tribute or rebelled outright. The Hittites, a powerful kingdom in Anatolia, were expanding southward, threatening Egyptian interests. The kingdom of Mitanni, which had been Egypt's ally, was weakening and would soon collapse. The careful diplomatic balance that had kept the region stable during Amenhotep III's reign was breaking down.

Within Egypt itself, there were signs of strain. The traditional priesthoods had been disbanded, but their wealth had been confiscated by the crown. This meant priests and temple employees had lost their livelihoods. The traditional festivals had ceased, disrupting the social and economic rhythms that had organized community life. The forced worship of the Aten, rather than the gods people had worshiped their entire lives, must have created resentment.

The later years of Akhenaten's reign are murky. Around year twelve or fourteen, something happened. We're not sure what. Nefertiti disappears from the record. Some scholars think she died, while others think she fell from favor. Some have suggested that she became co-regent under a different name. We simply don't know.

A figure named Smenkhkare appears in the records. She or he apparently served as co-regent with Akhenaten. Smenkhkare could have possibly been one of Akhenaten's daughters, but they also might have been a son we don't know about. It could even have been Nefertiti under a different name. Again, the evidence is frustratingly unclear.

By around year seventeen of his reign, Akhenaten died. The circumstances of his death are unknown. He was probably in his early thirties. He was buried at Amarna in a tomb cut into the cliffs east of the city, though his mummy has never been definitively identified.

Akhenaten's death left Egypt in a precarious position. The empire was weakening. The traditional religious establishment had been destroyed, but Atenism had not truly taken root. Egypt needed stability, and Akhenaten's immediate successors would struggle to provide it.

Chapter 10:
The Boy King and the General

Tutankhamun: Famous for Being Forgotten

Of all the pharaohs who ruled Egypt for three thousand years, none is more famous today than Tutankhamun. His golden death mask is one of the most recognizable images in the world. His name is synonymous with ancient Egypt in popular culture. Museums that display his artifacts draw enormous crowds. Movies, documentaries, and books about him appear regularly.

The irony is that Tutankhamun's reign was brief and, particularly in its early years, when he was very young, he served largely as a figurehead. The decisions were made by his advisors. While recent scholarship leaves open the possibility that he might have played a more active role in restoration policies as he grew older, his reign was spent primarily undoing his predecessor's religious revolution and trying to restore stability to Egypt. He never led a major military campaign. He contributed to some temple construction at sites like Karnak and Luxor, though these works were often modest compared to other pharaohs and were frequently usurped by his successors. By ancient Egyptian standards, his accomplishments were limited.

Tutankhamun's fame rests entirely on one fact: his tomb survived largely intact until its discovery in 1922, making it the most complete royal burial ever found from ancient Egypt.

Tutankhamun's famous golden death mask.[31]

When Tutankhamun came to the throne around 1332 BCE (taking the name Tutankhaten initially, later changed to Tutankhamun), he was probably around eight or nine years old, making him far too young to actually rule. Real power lay with his advisors, particularly Ay, an elderly official who had served under Akhenaten, and Horemheb, a powerful military commander who had risen to prominence during the Amarna period.

These men faced a difficult situation. Akhenaten's religious revolution had disrupted Egyptian society, weakened the empire, and created instability. The worship of traditional gods had been suppressed for nearly two decades. Egypt's international standing had declined since Akhenaten had neglected foreign policy and military affairs. The new capital at Amarna lacked the legitimacy and infrastructure of traditional centers like Thebes and Memphis.

The solution was clear: restore the old order. Within the first few years of Tutankhamun's reign, dramatic changes occurred. The court abandoned Amarna and returned to Memphis and Thebes. The traditional gods were restored to prominence. Temples were reopened and repaired. Priesthoods were reinstated, and festivals resumed. The young king's name was changed from Tutankhaten ("living image of the Aten") to Tutankhamun ("living image of Amun"), symbolizing the return to the traditional religion.

A text known as the Restoration Stela, erected at Karnak, describes the situation and the restoration: "Now when his majesty appeared as king, the temples of the gods and goddesses from Elephantine down to the marshes of the Delta had gone to pieces. Their shrines had become desolate, had become mounds overgrown with weeds ... The land was topsy-turvy, and the gods turned their backs upon this land."

The text is propaganda, of course, as it exaggerates the chaos to make the restoration seem more dramatic and necessary. However, it shows how those who came after Akhenaten viewed his reign—as a disaster that had to be corrected.

As Tutankhamun grew into his teens, he might have begun to exercise more personal authority, though we have little evidence of this. Royal inscriptions from his reign are conventional, showing him in traditional pharaonic poses—worshiping gods, smiting enemies, and receiving tribute. These images tell us little about what he actually did or thought.

We do know some personal details about Tutankhamun from his tomb and from analysis of his mummy. He was slightly built, about 5'6" tall. Medical examination has revealed various health issues. He had a clubfoot on his left leg that would have caused him to walk with a limp. He suffered from malaria (DNA evidence of the parasite was found in his remains), and he likely had other genetic issues from generations of royal inbreeding. His parents were likely full siblings. Genetic analysis suggests his father was Akhenaten and that his mother was one of Akhenaten's sisters.

Tutankhamun was married to Ankhesenamun, one of Akhenaten's daughters (and thus probably his half-sister). The couple apparently had two daughters, both stillborn or dying shortly after birth. The mummified fetuses were found in Tutankhamun's tomb. They were placed in small coffins.

Around 1323 BCE, Tutankhamun died. He was approximately eighteen or nineteen years old. The cause of death has been debated extensively, generating numerous theories over the years. Early theories suggested he was murdered. A blow to the back of the head visible in early

X-rays suggested violence. However, more recent CT scans have shown this damage was likely caused during the mummification process or by modern handling, not by an ancient blow.

Current medical consensus, based on extensive study of his mummy, suggests he died from a combination of factors. He had a broken leg; the femur of his left leg was fractured shortly before death. The break might have become infected. Combined with his existing health problems (malaria, possible immune issues from genetic disorders, and his clubfoot), an infected wound could have been fatal. While this is the leading theory, other medical hypotheses continue to be discussed, though diagnosing ancient diseases from mummified remains is challenging.

Some scholars suggest he might have fallen from a chariot, though this is speculative. What's clear is that his death was probably not murder but rather the result of health complications in a young man with multiple underlying conditions. In an era before antibiotics, a broken leg leading to infection could easily be fatal, even for a king.

Tutankhamun's death created a succession crisis. He had no surviving children. His widow, Ankhesenamun, was left without an heir. Who would succeed?

A remarkable letter survives in Hittite records, supposedly sent by an Egyptian queen to the Hittite king Suppiluliuma I. The letter writer (probably Ankhesenamun, though not named) asks the Hittite king to send one of his sons to Egypt to marry her and become pharaoh. She writes that her husband has died, that she has no sons, and that she needs a husband.

The Hittite king, suspicious of this unprecedented request, sent an envoy to investigate. Eventually, he agreed and sent a son. However, the Hittite prince never reached Egypt. He was killed, possibly by Egyptian officials opposed to a foreign king.

Whether this story is true or not, what's clear is that the succession was contested. Ay, the elderly advisor, became pharaoh after Tutankhamun. Some artifacts, such as a ring bearing both their names, suggest Ay might have married Ankhesenamun to legitimize his claim to the throne, though there is no definitive evidence of this marriage. Ay's reign was very brief—only about four years—before Horemheb, the military commander, took the throne.

Tutankhamun was buried in a small tomb in the Valley of the Kings, the necropolis where New Kingdom pharaohs were interred. The tomb was probably not originally intended for him. It's unusually small for a royal burial, suggesting it might have been a private tomb that was hastily repurposed when the king died unexpectedly.

The tomb consists of just four rooms: an entrance corridor, an antechamber, a burial chamber, and a small treasury. The burial was rushed. The paint in the burial chamber was still wet when the tomb was sealed, as fingerprints are visible in the paint. Some of the grave goods were recycled from earlier burials, with the names altered. The gold coffins show signs of hasty modification. Everything suggests that Tutankhamun's death was unexpected and that the burial had to be arranged quickly.

But despite the haste and the small tomb, Tutankhamun was buried with incredible wealth. The four small rooms were packed with grave goods: three nested coffins (the innermost of solid gold), a stone sarcophagus, furniture, chariots, weapons, jewelry, clothing, food, wine, oils, cosmetics, and countless other objects—over five thousand items in total.

The relief carving on one of the coffins featuring Tutankhamun and Ankhesenamun.[2]

The tomb was robbed twice in antiquity, shortly after it was sealed. Robbers tunneled through the blocked doorway, ransacked parts of the tomb, and made off with valuable items (particularly oils and unguents (a type of ointment), which were worth their weight in gold). But they were apparently caught or scared away before they could complete the robbery. Officials resealed the tomb, and it disappeared from memory.

Several factors probably contributed to the tomb being forgotten. Tutankhamun's reign was short and occurred during a controversial period that later pharaohs wanted to forget. His tomb entrance was small and unremarkable. Later pharaohs, particularly Ramesses VI, built tombs nearby, and debris from their construction covered Tutankhamun's entrance. Workers building Ramesses VI's tomb even built stone huts directly over Tutankhamun's buried entrance, not realizing there was a tomb beneath.

For over three thousand years, Tutankhamun's tomb lay undisturbed and forgotten, its entrance hidden beneath rubble and huts, while tomb robbers systematically plundered every other royal tomb in the valley.

On November 4th, 1922, British archaeologist Howard Carter, working in the Valley of the Kings under the patronage of Lord Carnarvon, discovered a stone step cut into the bedrock. Over the next few days, his team uncovered a staircase leading to a sealed doorway bearing Tutankhamun's name.

On November 26th, Carter made a small hole in the second sealed doorway and peered inside by candlelight. Lord Carnarvon asked, "Can you see anything?" Carter's reply became famous: "Yes, wonderful things."

The tomb was intact—or at least as intact as it had been after the ancient robberies. The antechamber was packed with objects. The burial chamber contained the king's nested coffins and sarcophagus. The treasury held the canopic shrine with the king's internal organs and countless other precious items.

It took Carter and his team ten years to carefully remove, catalog, and conserve all the objects. The discovery created a worldwide sensation. Newspapers covered it extensively. The public became fascinated with "King Tut." The beautiful objects, especially the golden death mask, captured people's imaginations. There was even talk of a "curse of the pharaohs" when Lord Carnarvon died a few months after the tomb's opening (he died from an infected mosquito bite—nothing supernatural, but the press loved the story).

The treasures from Tutankhamun's tomb have toured the world in various exhibitions, drawing millions of visitors. The golden death mask has become an icon of ancient Egypt and is instantly recognizable around the globe. Tutankhamun, who was virtually unknown before 1922, became the most famous pharaoh in the world.

It's precisely because his reign was brief and relatively insignificant that his tomb was small, easily overlooked, and survived. If Tutankhamun had been a more successful pharaoh—if he'd lived longer, built grand monuments, and conducted great campaigns—his tomb would probably have been larger, more conspicuous, and long since plundered like all the rest.

Tutankhamun is famous for being forgotten.

Horemheb and the Erasure of Amarna

After Ay's brief four-year reign, power passed to Horemheb (approximately 1319–1292 BCE, ruling for about twenty-seven years). He was a general who had served under both Akhenaten and Tutankhamun but who had no royal blood whatsoever. He was a commoner who rose to the throne through military power and political skill. His reign would mark the final end of the Amarna period and the thorough erasure of its memory.

Horemheb's background was in the military. He had served in the Egyptian army, rising through the ranks to become a general. During Tutankhamun's reign, he held the title "Commander of the Army" and was one of the most powerful men in Egypt. When Ay died without a clear heir, Horemheb was positioned to seize power, and he did.

His lack of royal lineage could have been a problem. Egyptian ideology emphasized the divine nature of kingship and the importance of royal bloodlines. But Horemheb handled this cleverly. He legitimized his rule by marrying Mutnedjmet, who was possibly Nefertiti's sister, which gave him a tenuous connection to the royal family. He also presented himself as chosen by the gods. Inscriptions describe how the god Horus selected Horemheb to be king, taking him by the hand and leading him to the throne.

However, legitimacy through divine selection and marriage wasn't enough. Horemheb needed to demonstrate that he could restore ma'at to Egypt. His reign focused on internal reform, the restoration of the traditional religion, and—most dramatically—the erasure of the Amarna period from history.

Horemheb's first priority was administrative reform. Egypt's bureaucracy and legal system had become corrupt and inefficient during the Amarna period. Horemheb issued a long decree, preserved on a stela at Karnak, outlining reforms to address various problems: corrupt officials extorting bribes, soldiers illegally seizing goods from civilians, dishonest tax collectors, and other abuses.

The decree specifies punishments for various crimes, many involving cutting off the nose or ears of offenders or, for serious crimes, execution. It's a harsh document, but it shows how Horemheb tried to restore order and honest administration to a system that had broken down.

He also reorganized the army, strengthening royal control over the military forces. He appointed officials based on merit rather than simply relying on hereditary positions. He worked to rebuild Egypt's international standing. While there's limited evidence of major military campaigns during his reign, some inscriptions suggest military activity in Nubia and Syria, though not on the same scale as earlier warrior pharaohs.

But Horemheb's most lasting impact was his systematic erasure of the Amarna period. He went further than Tutankhamun's restoration of the traditional religion, as he tried to erase all memory of Akhenaten, Smenkhkare, Tutankhamun, and Ay.

Their names were removed from the king lists. In official records, Egyptian history jumped directly from Amenhotep III to Horemheb, as if the intervening reigns had never occurred. Horemheb even dated his own reign from the death of Amenhotep III, claiming all the years back to that point as his own.

Monuments bearing the names of the Amarna pharaohs were defaced. Cartouches were chiseled out. Statues were destroyed or usurped (meaning Horemheb had his own names carved on them). Temples built during the Amarna period were dismantled, their stone blocks reused in new constructions where the blocks would be hidden, literally burying the memory of the heretics.

A statue of Horemheb with the god Amun.[38]

Amarna itself was abandoned. Without royal patronage, the city quickly declined. People moved away, and buildings fell into disrepair. The desert began to reclaim the site. Within a few decades of its founding, Akhenaten's grand capital was a ghost town, slowly disappearing beneath sand and debris.

Why such thorough erasure? The Amarna period represented multiple violations of Egyptian ideological principles. Akhenaten had rejected the traditional gods, threatening the cosmic order. His religious revolution had weakened Egypt internally and internationally. The entire period was seen as a time when Egypt had strayed from ma'at, when the proper order had been violated, and when chaos had threatened to overcome civilization.

By erasing all records of this period, Horemheb was symbolically undoing the damage, pretending it had never happened. In Egyptian belief, if something wasn't recorded or if a name wasn't preserved, it ceased to exist in any meaningful way. By removing the names and records, Horemheb was attempting to unmake the Amarna period, to remove it from history and from cosmic reality.

The erasure was remarkably successful. For centuries, Akhenaten and Tutankhamun were largely forgotten in official records and memory, though some objects bearing their names survived in obscure locations. They appeared in no king lists. Their monuments were destroyed or hidden. Their names survived only in a few obscure references that later generations couldn't interpret.

When Greek and Roman travelers visited Egypt, they saw no record of these pharaohs. It was only in the 19th century CE, when archaeologists began systematically exploring Egypt, that the Amarna period was rediscovered. The ruins of Amarna were excavated, and the Amarna letters were found and translated. Tutankhamun's tomb was discovered intact. The cartouches that Horemheb's workers had chiseled out were still recognizable enough to be read. Slowly, the erased period came back into view, rescued from the oblivion to which ancient Egyptians had consigned it.

Horemheb ruled for approximately twenty-seven years, dying around 1292 BCE. His reign marked the end of the Eighteenth Dynasty. He apparently designated his vizier, Ramesses, as his successor, though this designation is not recorded in contemporary inscriptions and likely occurred near the end of his reign. This Ramesses would become Ramesses I, founder of the Nineteenth Dynasty.

The Nineteenth Dynasty would see Egypt return to military glory under kings like Seti I and Ramesses II. The Egyptian empire would be restored. Grand monuments would be built. Egypt would once again be a dominant power in the Near East. The disruptions of the Amarna period would become a distant memory, hidden so well that even most ancient Egyptians forgot they had ever happened.

In the modern era, the Amarna period has become one of the most studied periods in all of Egyptian history. Akhenaten is seen as one of history's most fascinating figures. Tutankhamun is the most famous pharaoh in the world. Nefertiti's bust is one of the most recognizable images from ancient Egypt. The period Horemheb tried so hard to erase has become, ironically, one of the most famous periods of Egyptian history. Memory is harder to kill than Horemheb imagined, and the period he tried to forget has refused to stay forgotten.

The famous bust of Nefertiti.³⁴

Chapter 11: The Ramessides—
Last Gasp of Greatness

Ramesses II: Egypt's Greatest Showman

After the chaos of the Amarna period and Horemheb's restoration, Egypt needed strong leadership to rebuild its power and prestige. That leadership came from the Nineteenth Dynasty, which was founded by Ramesses I around 1292 BCE. Ramesses I's reign was brief—only about two years—but he established a new royal line that would dominate Egypt for over a century.

Real power passed quickly to his son, Seti I (approximately 1290–1279 BCE), who would prove to be one of the New Kingdom's most effective rulers. Seti inherited an Egypt that had survived the Amarna crisis but had lost much of its international standing. The empire in Syria–Palestine had weakened. Seti set about reversing these losses through military campaigns and ambitious building projects.

Seti I was a warrior pharaoh in the traditional sense. He campaigned extensively in Syria–Palestine, reasserting Egyptian control over territories that had slipped away during the Amarna period. He fought against the Hittites for control of strategic cities in Syria. He campaigned in Libya to secure Egypt's western border. His military activities restored Egyptian power and sent a clear message: Egypt was back, and its pharaoh was once again a force to be reckoned with.

However, Seti I wasn't just a warrior; he was also a prolific builder. His greatest monument is his mortuary temple at Abydos, one of the most beautiful temples in Egypt. The temple features some of the finest relief carvings from ancient Egypt, with detailed scenes showing Seti offering tribute to the gods. The reliefs are so precisely carved and so well preserved that they remain breathtaking nearly three thousand years later.

Seti I's mortuary temple.[35]

At Abydos, Seti carved the famous Abydos King List, a chronological list of Egyptian pharaohs from the First Dynasty to his own reign. Notably, the list omits the Amarna pharaohs—Akhenaten, Smenkhkare, Tutankhamun, and Ay—jumping directly from Amenhotep III to Horemheb.

Seti's tomb in the Valley of the Kings is the longest and deepest royal tomb ever constructed there, stretching over four hundred feet into the bedrock. Its walls are covered with religious texts and images guiding the king through the afterlife. The tomb's artistic quality is exceptional, and it remains one of ancient Egypt's most impressive underground monuments.

The interior of Seti I's tomb.[36]

Near the end of his reign, Seti elevated his young son as co-regent, ensuring a smooth succession and allowing the prince to gain experience. When Seti I died around 1279 BCE after ruling for approximately eleven to fifteen years (chronologies vary), his son was ready to take full power. That son would become Ramesses II—and he would rule Egypt for sixty-six years, one of the longest reigns in history.

Ramesses II inherited a stable, prosperous kingdom from his capable father. Egypt's economy was strong. The army was well trained and well equipped. The administration functioned smoothly. International relations were generally good, though there was ongoing tension with the Hittite Empire to the north over control of Syria. Seti I had restored Egypt's power; Ramesses II would take that foundation and build something even more spectacular, at least in terms of visibility and self-promotion.

By the time Ramesses II had died in 1213 BCE, he had fathered over one hundred children with various wives and concubines. He had overseen one of the largest building programs in Egyptian history. His colossal statues stood throughout Egypt. His name appeared everywhere, carved on structures both old and new. He had fought dramatic battles, signed one of the ancient world's most famous peace treaties, and presided over Egypt during decades of prosperity and stability.

Ramesses II wasn't necessarily Egypt's most successful military commander or its most effective administrator, but he was undeniably its most visible ruler. Three thousand years later, when people think of ancient Egypt, they often think of Ramesses, whether it's his massive statues, his grand temples, or his larger-than-life presence.

He's sometimes called Ramesses the Great, and in terms of fame and monument-building, the title fits. But the reality behind the propaganda is more complex. Early in his reign, Ramesses followed his father's example, conducting military campaigns in Syria–Palestine to maintain Egyptian influence. These early campaigns were mostly successful. They were small-scale operations against rebellious vassals or troublesome groups—the normal business of maintaining an empire.

Then came the Battle of Kadesh, the event that Ramesses would commemorate more extensively than any other achievement of his reign.

Ramesses defeating a foe during the Battle of Kadesh.[37]

In his fifth year as pharaoh (around 1274 BCE), Ramesses led a major military expedition north into Syria to confront the Hittite Empire. The Hittites, based in Anatolia (modern Turkey), had been expanding southward and competing with Egypt for control over the wealthy cities of Syria–Palestine. The city of Kadesh, located in what is now Syria near the modern Lebanese border, was a strategic prize. Controlling Kadesh meant controlling important trade routes.

Ramesses marched north with four divisions of the Egyptian army, perhaps sixteen thousand to twenty thousand men in total. The Hittite king Muwatalli II had assembled his own forces, including troops from allied kingdoms throughout Anatolia and Syria. He possibly commanded a similar or even larger number.

What happened at Kadesh is documented in extraordinary detail by the Egyptians. Ramesses had the story carved on temple walls throughout Egypt, accompanied by dramatic images. The account appears at the Ramesseum (Ramesses's mortuary temple), at Abu Simbel, at Karnak, at Luxor, and at Abydos. It's one of the most extensively documented battles in ancient history, at least from one side's perspective.

According to the Egyptian account, Ramesses was tricked by Hittite spies posing as deserters, who told him the Hittite army was far to the north, near Aleppo. Believing this false intelligence, Ramesses advanced quickly with just his first division, the Amun division, leaving his other three divisions strung out behind him along the route.

As Ramesses camped northwest of Kadesh, the Hittite army, which had actually been hiding nearby, launched a surprise attack. They struck the Ra division, the second Egyptian division that was still on the march south of Kadesh, catching it completely unprepared. The Ra division broke and fled in panic toward Ramesses's camp.

The Hittite chariot force then swept into Ramesses's camp itself. The Egyptian soldiers panicked. Officers fled. The situation looked desperate. The pharaoh was surrounded by enemy forces, his army scattered and demoralized, facing defeat and possibly capture or death.

This is where Ramesses's account becomes particularly dramatic. According to the text, Ramesses found himself abandoned by his soldiers. He was alone except for his chariot driver. He prayed to the god Amun, reproaching the god for allowing this to happen after all Ramesses had done for him. Amun responded, promising to give Ramesses the strength of thousands.

Inspired by divine intervention, Ramesses single-handedly charged into the Hittite forces. The texts describe him cutting through enemy ranks like a whirlwind, his arrows never missing, his enemies falling before him. He made six individual charges through the Hittite forces, each time emerging victorious. The enemy was so terrified of his prowess that they threw themselves into the river to escape him.

Eventually, the Ptah division arrived from the south, and then another Egyptian force arrived—possibly the Ne'arin, though the identity of this force remains debated among scholars. The Hittites withdrew across the river. Ramesses had achieved a miraculous victory through his own valor and divine favor.

That's the Egyptian version. It's heroic, dramatic, and makes for great propaganda. However, it's clearly exaggerated, and we can read between the lines to understand what probably actually happened.

The Hittites clearly had a tactical surprise and initially had the upper hand. The Egyptian army was caught unprepared and took heavy losses. Ramesses probably did personally fight—Egyptian pharaohs were expected to lead from the front, and Ramesses seems to have been genuinely brave. But the claim that he single-handedly fought off the entire Hittite army is blatant propaganda.

What likely saved the Egyptians was the arrival of reinforcements—the Ptah division and the additional force—which turned a potential disaster into a chaotic but not catastrophic engagement. The Hittites withdrew, though the reasons for their withdrawal remain unclear. It might have been tactical rather than fear of Egyptian strength.

The next day, according to Egyptian sources, there was more fighting, but it was inconclusive. After this, Ramesses withdrew south, leaving Kadesh in Hittite hands.

Yes, the Hittites kept Kadesh. Egypt didn't achieve its strategic objective of securing the city. Egyptian casualties were significant. By any objective military standard, this wasn't a victory.

However, Ramesses proclaimed it as his greatest triumph. He commissioned texts and reliefs showing his heroic stand. He had poets compose epic accounts of the battle. He made Kadesh the defining moment of his military career, proof of his divine favor and personal courage.

This wasn't unusual for ancient rulers. Spinning military defeats or inconclusive battles as victories was a common practice. But Ramesses took it to an extreme. The sheer volume of inscriptions and reliefs commemorating Kadesh is remarkable. If you visited Egyptian temples in antiquity, you couldn't escape the story of how Ramesses heroically saved Egypt at Kadesh.

An original relief of the Battle of Kadesh in the Ramesseum.[38]

After Kadesh, Ramesses continued campaigning in Syria–Palestine for another decade or so, but without any decisive breakthrough. Neither the Egyptians nor the Hittites could gain a clear advantage. The two powers were roughly equal in strength, and the cost of continued warfare was becoming unsustainable for both.

Around 1259 BCE, about fifteen years after Kadesh, Ramesses and the Hittite king Hattusili III signed a peace treaty. The treaty, recorded in both Egyptian hieroglyphics and Hittite cuneiform, is the first and most comprehensive peace treaty from the ancient world. A copy hangs in the United Nations headquarters in New York as a symbol of early international diplomacy.

The treaty established peace between Egypt and the Hittites, defined their respective spheres of influence in Syria–Palestine, established mutual defense provisions (if either kingdom was attacked by a third party, the other would provide military assistance), and even included extradition provisions for fugitives who fled from one kingdom to the other.

The treaty was sealed by a diplomatic marriage. Ramesses married a Hittite princess, the daughter of Hattusili III. Later, he married another Hittite princess. These marriages helped maintain peace between the two powers for the rest of Ramesses's reign.

The treaty worked remarkably well. Egypt and the Hittite Empire maintained peaceful relations. They corresponded regularly; letters between the Egyptian and Hittite courts survive. They coordinated on diplomatic matters. The costly warfare in Syria came to an end.

This peace allowed Ramesses to focus on what he's most famous for: building.

Ramesses II oversaw one of the largest building programs in Egyptian history. The scale and number of his construction projects were unprecedented, though much of his building projects involved usurping earlier monuments—having his name carved on statues and structures built by previous pharaohs or recycling and re-inscribing monuments from earlier reigns. He built new temples, expanded existing ones, and ensured his name appeared on monuments throughout Egypt.

His most famous monument is Abu Simbel in Nubia, far south of Egypt proper. This temple, carved directly into a cliff face, features four colossal seated statues of Ramesses at its entrance, each about sixty-seven feet tall. Inside, the temple contains halls with more statues and reliefs. Twice a year, on specific dates aligned with the solar year, sunlight penetrates deep into the temple to illuminate statues in the inner sanctuary—a remarkable feat of ancient engineering and astronomical knowledge.

Abu Simbel also features a smaller temple dedicated to Ramesses's favorite wife, Nefertari, with statues of her standing alongside the king, which is unusual recognition for a queen. The temple's inscriptions proclaim Ramesses's greatness and his divine status.

The Temple of Ramesses II on the left and the Small Temple of Hathor and Nefertari on the right.[19]

In the 1960s, when the construction of the Aswan High Dam threatened to submerge Abu Simbel under Lake Nasser, an international effort organized by UNESCO dismantled the entire temple complex and moved it to higher ground, cutting it into blocks and reassembling it exactly as it had been. It was one of the most ambitious archaeological rescue operations ever undertaken.

Moving the colossal statues.[30]

Ramesses also built the Ramesseum, his massive mortuary temple on the west bank at Thebes. The complex covered an enormous territory and included a temple, palace, storage magazines, and administrative buildings. The Ramesseum once featured a colossal seated statue of Ramesses weighing over one thousand tons, making it one of the largest statues ever carved in ancient Egypt. It now lies in broken pieces. This statue inspired Percy Bysshe Shelley's famous poem "Ozymandias" (Ozymandias being a Greek rendering of one of Ramesses's throne names). The poem's ironic meditation on the impermanence of power and pride is particularly fitting for Ramesses, the king who built so much to ensure his eternal fame.

At Karnak, Ramesses completed the massive hypostyle hall begun by his father Seti I. The hall contains 134 enormous columns, some reaching 70 feet high, their capitals carved in the form of papyrus flowers. The hall is so large that Notre-Dame Cathedral in Paris could fit inside it. While Seti I started this project, Ramesses finished and decorated it, ensuring his name appeared prominently throughout.

The Great Hypostyle Hall.[81]

At Luxor Temple, Ramesses added a new court and pylon entrance, along with six colossal statues of himself and two obelisks (one now stands in the Place de la Concorde in Paris, as it was given to France in the 19th century).

He built temples at Memphis, at Abydos, throughout the Nile Delta, and in Nubia. Everywhere he built, colossal statues of Ramesses dominated the landscape. His cartouches appeared on walls, columns, and doorways. His building program employed thousands of workers, including quarrymen, transporters, sculptors, painters, architects, and administrators.

Why did he build so much? Multiple reasons. Building temples honored the gods and maintained ma'at. It demonstrated the pharaoh's power and wealth. It provided employment and stimulated the economy. It ensured the pharaoh's name would be remembered—and Ramesses was clearly obsessed with ensuring his eternal fame. Building also served as propaganda, impressing Egyptians and foreigners with Egypt's might and the pharaoh's divine status.

Ramesses's family life was equally on a grand scale. He had numerous wives, the most important being Nefertari, whom he married early in his reign and who appears to have been his favorite. She bore several of his children and was honored with her own temple at Abu Simbel and a beautifully decorated tomb in the Valley of the Queens. It is one of the most stunning tombs in ancient Egypt, with vibrant painted reliefs that remain remarkably well preserved.

Horus leading Nefertari by the hand.[32]

After Nefertari's death, Ramesses elevated another wife, Isetnofret, to chief queen. He also married at least one of his own daughters, Bintanath, and possibly a second daughter, Nebettawy. This practice became more common in the later New Kingdom, perhaps influenced by the royal inbreeding of earlier periods or as a way to reinforce royal bloodlines.

Ramesses fathered over one hundred children—some sources say as many as 150, though exact numbers are uncertain. With so many offspring, the succession became complicated. His sons were given ranks, with the eldest being designated crown prince. However, Ramesses lived to around ninety in an era when life expectancy was perhaps thirty-five to forty years, outliving many of his sons. His first dozen sons died before him, and the throne eventually passed to Merneptah, who was the thirteenth son in the official procession lists but the fourth to be designated crown prince due to the deaths of his older brothers. Merneptah was already elderly when he became pharaoh.

Ramesses was an old man when he died. His mummy shows evidence of arthritis, dental problems, and other age-related conditions. However, he remained active, continuing to oversee building projects and administration in his later years.

When he finally died in 1213 BCE, his passing marked the end of an era. He had ruled for so long that most Egyptians had known no other pharaoh. His reign had been prosperous and stable. Egypt had been at peace with major powers like the Hittites, though smaller campaigns continued in Nubia and Libya. The temples were full, the granaries stocked, and the borders secure.

Ramesses II had achieved his goal of eternal fame. His monuments still stand, and his name is known worldwide. He represents ancient Egypt in popular imagination—the powerful pharaoh surrounded by colossal statues and grand temples.

But beneath the propaganda and the monuments, was Ramesses actually a great pharaoh? The evidence is mixed. He signed a treaty that essentially recognized the status quo rather than achieving military dominance. His building projects, while impressive, relied heavily on usurpation and consumed vast resources that would strain Egypt's economy in the decades after his death. His extremely long reign, while stable, meant that an elderly son would inherit, potentially creating succession difficulties.

Ramesses was a master of image management, a pharaoh who understood that appearing powerful could be as important as actually being powerful. He was Egypt's greatest showman. And in ancient Egypt, where the pharaoh was both king and god, where maintaining ma'at required projecting divine authority, showmanship mattered. Whether that makes him "great" depends on how you define greatness.

The Sea Peoples and the Bronze Age Collapse

Around the time of Ramesses II's death and in the decades that followed, the entire eastern Mediterranean world began to collapse. Great kingdoms and civilizations that had existed for centuries suddenly fell. Cities burned, and trade networks disintegrated. Literacy declined or disappeared. Populations decreased dramatically. Archaeologists call this period the Bronze Age Collapse. It was one of the most catastrophic civilizational breakdowns in human history.

Egypt survived this collapse as a unified state, unlike the Hittites or the Mycenaeans, but it lost its entire empire in Syria–Palestine, suffered massive economic disruption, and became significantly weakened. And playing a major role in this chaos were mysterious groups collectively known as the Sea Peoples.

The Bronze Age world of the late 13th and early 12th centuries BCE was highly interconnected. The great powers—Egypt, the Hittites, Mycenaean Greece, Assyria, Babylon, and the kingdoms of Syria–Palestine—traded extensively with each other. Tin from Afghanistan reached the Mediterranean. Copper from Cyprus was worked into bronze throughout the region. Grain from Egypt fed populations far away. Luxury goods, like ivory, incense, precious metals, and dyed textiles, moved along established trade routes.

This world was also interconnected. The great powers communicated diplomatically in Akkadian, the international language. They exchanged gifts and ambassadors. They made treaties and arranged royal marriages. They maintained a balance of power that, while not without conflict, provided relative stability.

Then, starting around 1200 BCE, this world fell apart rather quickly.

The Hittite Empire, which had been Egypt's rival and then its ally, collapsed completely. Its capital, Hattusa, was burned and abandoned. The empire fragmented, and Hittite civilization essentially disappeared from history. The collapse resulted from a combination of factors: severe famines documented in texts, internal political strife, drought, and systemic administrative failure. The groups identified as Sea Peoples might have moved through these already destabilized regions, possibly delivering final blows to territories where Hittite control had already broken down. Where there had been a great power controlling Anatolia and northern Syria, there was suddenly chaos.

The Mycenaean palaces of Greece—centers of the Bronze Age Greek civilization that would later inspire stories of the Trojan War—were destroyed. Most major sites were abandoned or saw only limited later occupation. The elaborate palace-based civilization of Mycenaean Greece vanished, and Greece entered a dark age that would last several centuries.

Cities throughout the eastern Mediterranean were destroyed. Archaeological excavations show dramatic layers of destruction at sites across the region—Ugarit in Syria, Megiddo in Palestine, Hazor in Palestine, and many others. These weren't slow declines but sudden, violent destructions.

Trade networks collapsed. The supply of tin, essential for making bronze, was disrupted. The copper trade from Cyprus ceased. The interconnected economy that had supported the Bronze Age civilizations broke down.

What caused this catastrophe? This question has fascinated and frustrated scholars for decades, and there's still no consensus. The collapse was almost certainly caused by multiple factors working together.

One factor was the groups collectively called the Sea Peoples. Egyptian sources from the reigns of Merneptah (Ramesses II's son and successor) and Ramesses III describe attacks by foreign invaders coming by both sea and land. Egyptian texts list various distinct groups with names like the Peleset, Tjeker, Shekelesh, Denyen, and Weshesh. Modern scholars collectively call these groups the Sea Peoples, though this is a modern term. The ancient sources don't use this exact phrase and instead identify separate groups moving through the region.

Who were the Sea Peoples? We still don't really know. The Egyptian texts don't provide much detail about their origins or society. Some groups might have come from Anatolia, others possibly from the Aegean or Greece, others from Sicily or Sardinia (some of the names have been tentatively connected to later peoples in these regions; for instance, the Peleset are widely believed to be related to the later Philistines, though this connection is not proven). They might have been displaced populations fleeing disasters in their homelands, opportunistic raiders taking advantage of the chaos, or something else entirely.

What we do know is that they appeared in large numbers moving through the eastern Mediterranean. Egyptian reliefs show them with their families, ox-carts loaded with possessions, suggesting they weren't just raiders but displaced peoples looking for new lands.

In Merneptah's fifth year (around 1208 BCE), Egypt faced a major invasion from the west. A Libyan chief named Meryey allied with several Sea Peoples groups and invaded the western Nile Delta with a large force—perhaps tens of thousands of warriors and their families. They apparently hoped to settle in the fertile delta region.

Merneptah, despite being elderly (he had become pharaoh in his fifties after Ramesses II's extremely long reign), responded. He assembled the Egyptian army and met the invaders in battle somewhere in the western delta. The Egyptian account describes a decisive victory. Over six thousand enemies were killed, many more captured, and Meryey fled back to Libya.

An inscription from Merneptah's reign celebrating this victory, known as the Merneptah Stela, is notable for another reason: it contains the earliest known reference to "Israel" outside the Bible. The stela lists various defeated enemies, including a group called Israel located in Canaan, though it tells us nothing else about them.

Merneptah's victory secured Egypt against the immediate threat, but it didn't end the larger crisis. The Sea Peoples continued to move through the eastern Mediterranean, and the collapse of other civilizations continued.

The most detailed Egyptian account of the Sea Peoples comes from the reign of Ramesses III (c. 1186-1155 BCE), who ruled early in the Twentieth Dynasty, about a generation after Merneptah. Ramesses III faced multiple threats during his reign and recorded his victories in detailed reliefs and inscriptions at his mortuary temple at Medinet Habu.

According to these texts and reliefs, in Ramesses III's fifth and eighth years (around 1180 and 1177 BCE), Egypt faced massive invasions by the Sea Peoples. The invaders moved through Syria–Palestine toward Egypt, through regions that had already been destabilized and fragmented following the collapse of major powers. They came by both land (moving down the coast with their families and possessions) and sea (in ships carrying warriors).

Ramesses III describes preparing Egypt's defenses. He fortified the mouths of the Nile and positioned army units along the coast. He also prepared the Egyptian navy to meet the seaborne invasion.

The reliefs at Medinet Habu show two major battles. The first was a land battle in Syria-Palestine or the Sinai, where Egyptian forces met the Sea Peoples' land army. The reliefs show Egyptian troops, including foreign mercenaries, fighting the invaders. The Egyptians claimed victory, with heaps of dead enemies and captives being taken.

The second was a naval battle, probably fought in the Nile Delta. This is depicted in remarkable detail in the reliefs—one of the few ancient Egyptian depictions of naval warfare. Egyptian ships engage Sea Peoples' vessels. Archers shoot from the ships. Men fall into the water. The Egyptian ships appear to be grappling and boarding enemy vessels. The Egyptians claimed a decisive victory, with enemy ships captured or sunk and large numbers of captives taken.

A sketch of the relief of the Battle of the Delta.[33]

Ramesses III's victories were genuine military successes, as they prevented the Sea Peoples from invading and settling in Egypt proper. Since the Sea Peoples didn't settle in Egypt itself, it is believed that the Egyptian defenses held.

However, the wars were costly. The disruption of trade networks hurt Egypt's economy. The collapse of neighboring kingdoms meant fewer trading partners. Egypt became more isolated as a result. Egyptian control over territories in Syria-Palestine was lost entirely. The empire contracted back to Egypt proper and Nubia.

Some of the Sea Peoples groups settled in areas that had been under Egyptian influence. The Peleset settled on the southern coast of Canaan in areas that would become the Philistine cities known in the Bible. Other groups settled elsewhere in the region. Egypt couldn't prevent this—Egyptian power was no longer what it had been.

What caused the Bronze Age Collapse beyond the Sea Peoples themselves? Scholars have proposed multiple contributing factors.

First off, evidence suggests the region experienced severe droughts around this time. Agricultural production would have declined, causing food shortages, economic stress, and population movements. The Sea Peoples themselves might have been climate refugees fleeing failed harvests in their homelands.

Archaeological evidence also shows earthquake damage at many sites during this period. A series of major earthquakes could have damaged cities and disrupted societies already stressed by other problems.

Some destroyed palaces show evidence suggesting internal violence rather than external attack. Popular uprisings against palace elites might have contributed to the collapse.

The Bronze Age civilizations were highly interconnected and dependent on each other for resources. When some parts of the system failed, there was a cascade effect. The collapse of the Hittites disrupted trade routes, which hurt other kingdoms, which affected still others, and so on.

Lastly, even if the Sea Peoples didn't cause the initial collapse, they certainly made it worse. As central authorities weakened, raiding became easier and more profitable. The movement of large groups of displaced peoples put additional stress on societies that were already struggling.

Most likely, the Bronze Age Collapse resulted from all these factors working together. It was a "perfect storm" that overwhelmed the resilience of Bronze Age civilizations.

A dark age descended on much of the eastern Mediterranean. Egypt survived as a unified state, but it was a diminished power in a more dangerous world. The great days of the New Kingdom were ending. Egypt would never again be the dominant power it had been under Thutmose III or even Ramesses II. The next several centuries would see a slow, uneven decline punctuated by occasional recoveries.

The End of an Era

After Ramesses III's victories against the Sea Peoples, Egypt had bought itself time, but the glory days were fading. The Twentieth Dynasty, to which Ramesses III belonged, would continue for several more decades, but each successive pharaoh was weaker than the last.

Ramesses III himself faced serious internal problems. Late in his reign, he survived an assassination plot. Court documents describe a conspiracy involving one of his wives and members of the royal household who plotted to kill him and place a different son on the throne. The conspiracy was discovered, and the plotters were tried and executed. However, the fact that such a conspiracy could occur showed the internal stresses Egypt was experiencing.

Some scholars believe Ramesses III might have actually been killed in the assassination attempt or died shortly after. Medical examination of his mummy revealed that his throat had been cut, possibly during the assassination. Whether he died immediately or survived to see the conspirators punished remains debated, but his death marked the beginning of the end for the Ramesside dynasty.

After Ramesses III, Egypt was ruled by a series of pharaohs, all named Ramesses (Ramesses IV through XI), who reigned in succession over the next century. These later Ramesses pharaohs are often difficult to distinguish from each other. Their reigns were short, their accomplishments limited, and their names chosen perhaps in hope of recapturing the glory of Ramesses II.

During these reigns, the decline of Egypt became increasingly obvious. Egypt's empire in Syria–Palestine was gone. The gold and tribute that had once flowed into Egypt from conquered territories dried up. The economy suffered.

Workers weren't being paid. One of the most remarkable documents from ancient Egypt dates to the reign of Ramesses III—a record of the first recorded labor strike in history. Workers building royal tombs in the Valley of the Kings stopped work and staged a sit-down strike because they hadn't been paid their rations. The fact that royal tomb workers—highly skilled craftsmen working on the most important religious monuments—weren't being paid shows serious economic problems.

The strikes became more frequent under later Ramesses pharaohs. Workers demonstrated, occupied temples, and refused to work until paid. The government struggled to supply basic rations. This wasn't because Egypt had become poor overnight. It was because the administrative system was breaking down. Resources weren't being distributed efficiently. Corruption was increasing. Central authority was weakening.

The power of the priesthood, particularly the priesthood of Amun at Thebes, was growing. As royal authority weakened, the priests of Amun, who controlled vast wealth, extensive lands, and thousands of temple workers, became increasingly independent. The high priest of Amun at Thebes was becoming nearly as powerful as the pharaoh, controlling southern Egypt almost as a separate kingdom.

Tomb robberies became epidemic during the later Twentieth Dynasty. The elaborate tombs in the Valley of the Kings, filled with treasures, were obvious targets. Organized gangs of tomb robbers plundered royal burials over several decades. Court records preserve trials of captured tomb robbers, who described tunneling into tombs, stripping mummies of their gold, and melting down precious objects. Even the tombs of pharaohs who had died just decades earlier were robbed.

The fact that royal tombs could be robbed on such a scale shows the breakdown of authority. These weren't opportunistic thefts but organized criminal enterprises, apparently involving corrupt officials who helped the robbers or looked the other way. The authorities caught some robbers and punished them harshly, but they couldn't stop the wave of robberies.

Military power was also declining. Egypt no longer had the resources or organization to conduct major campaigns. The army increasingly relied on foreign mercenaries, including Libyans and Nubians, who were less loyal to the Egyptian crown. These mercenaries sometimes settled in Egypt, particularly in the Nile Delta, creating foreign communities within Egyptian territory.

By the reign of Ramesses XI (roughly 1099–1069 BCE), the last pharaoh of the Twentieth Dynasty, central authority had effectively collapsed into divided power centers. Egypt was no longer unified under strong central control. In the south, the high priest of Amun at Thebes, a man named Herihor, effectively ruled as an independent king, even taking royal titles. In the north, another official named Smendes controlled the Nile Delta from the city of Tanis. Ramesses XI remained pharaoh in name, but he controlled little actual territory and had minimal authority.

This situation is sometimes called the "Renaissance Era" or the "Wehem Mesut" (meaning "Repeating of Births" or "Renaissance"), a term used in ancient texts suggesting an attempt at reform or renewal. However, it was really a recognition that the old order had collapsed and a new system was emerging.

Chapter 12:
The Third Intermediate Period —
Division and Foreign Rule

Egypt Splits in Two

When Ramesses XI died around 1069 BCE, Egypt entered what historians call the Third Intermediate Period—a time of political fragmentation that would last approximately 350 years. The unified kingdom that had existed since the start of the New Kingdom was no more. Instead, Egypt would be divided between competing power centers, ruled by dynasties of Libyan origin, briefly reunified by Nubian conquerors, and eventually invaded by the mighty Assyrian Empire.

This wasn't a sudden catastrophic collapse like the Bronze Age Collapse that had destroyed the Hittites and Mycenaeans. Egypt didn't experience mass destruction of cities or the loss of literacy. Egyptian culture remained vibrant. Temples still functioned, art and religious practices continued to flourish, and daily life for most Egyptians probably didn't change dramatically. However, the centralized political authority that had characterized the New Kingdom was gone. Egypt had fractured politically, even as its cultural traditions continued.

The division was already established before Ramesses XI's death. In the north, a man named Smendes ruled from the city of Tanis in the Nile Delta. When Ramesses XI died, Smendes claimed the title of pharaoh and established what historians call the Twenty-first Dynasty. He controlled Lower Egypt—the delta region and the area around Memphis.

In the south, the high priest of Amun at Thebes controlled Upper Egypt. Herihor, who had been high priest during the final years of Ramesses XI's reign, had already taken royal titles. After Ramesses XI's death, the high priests of Amun continued to rule southern Egypt as a virtual theocracy—a state controlled by religious authorities.

This division between north and south would persist, in various forms, for much of the Third Intermediate Period. Sometimes the division was cooperative, with the northern pharaoh and the southern high priest working together and intermarrying their families. Sometimes it was more hostile, with competition for resources and authority. Regardless, the unified Egypt of the New Kingdom was gone.

Why did Smendes rule from Tanis rather than from Memphis or Thebes, the traditional capitals? It was mostly for practical reasons. Tanis was located in the northeastern Nile Delta, close to the Mediterranean coast and to trade routes to the Levant. It was better positioned for commerce and communication with the outside world. Memphis and Thebes, while still important cities, were less central to the politics of the late 2nd millennium BCE.

Smendes and his successors of the Twenty-first Dynasty weren't particularly powerful. They ruled a diminished kingdom—just Lower Egypt and part of Middle Egypt. They had limited resources. They conducted no major military campaigns and built few monuments. They're known primarily from inscriptions and from finds at Tanis, where archaeologists discovered intact royal tombs in the 1930s and 1940s. These tombs were filled with beautiful objects, including silver coffins and golden masks, showing that the Twenty-first Dynasty pharaohs, while weak politically, still had access to considerable wealth.

The high priests of Amun controlled Upper Egypt. They commanded the wealth of the Amun temple complex at Karnak, one of the richest institutions in Egypt. They married into the royal family of the northern dynasty, maintaining ties. But they ruled independently, conducting their own administration, maintaining their own military forces, and generally acting as kings in all but name.

This situation—two separate power centers in Egypt—might seem strange, but it worked reasonably well for several generations. The Twenty-first Dynasty lasted about 130 years (roughly 1069–945 BCE), during which time Egypt avoided major conflicts and maintained relative stability, even if the kingdom was divided.

Then came the Libyans.

Libyans had been present in Egypt for centuries. They lived west of the Nile Valley in the desert regions. They had raided Egypt periodically, and Egyptian armies had fought against them. However, they had also served as mercenaries in the Egyptian army, and many Libyan families had settled in Egypt, particularly in the delta, over generations.

By the later Twenty-first Dynasty, many Libyans living in Egypt had become thoroughly Egyptianized. They had adopted Egyptian culture, worshiped Egyptian gods, and married into Egyptian families. These were not foreign invaders but assimilated military families whose ancestors had settled in Egypt generations earlier. They were Egyptian in culture, even if they were Libyan in ancestry.

One such family produced a man named Shoshenq, who served as a military commander under the last pharaohs of the Twenty-first Dynasty. Shoshenq was powerful, wealthy, and ambitious. When the last pharaoh of the Twenty-first Dynasty died around 945 BCE, Shoshenq claimed the throne, establishing the Twenty-second Dynasty.

Shoshenq I (ruled approximately 945–924 BCE) was the most powerful pharaoh Egypt had seen since the end of the New Kingdom. He reasserted authority over Egypt, bringing both the north and the south under his influence, though local elites, especially at Thebes, retained considerable autonomy. He placed his own sons in positions of power. One son became high priest of Amun at Thebes, ensuring southern loyalty. Another son governed key cities. Shoshenq was rebuilding centralized royal authority, even if his control wasn't absolute.

He also conducted military campaigns abroad, something Egyptian pharaohs hadn't done effectively for generations. Around 925 BCE, Shoshenq led an army into Palestine. Egyptian inscriptions record that he captured numerous cities in both the northern kingdom of Israel and the southern kingdom of Judah. This campaign appears in the Hebrew Bible—1 Kings 14:25–26 describes how "Shishak king of Egypt" attacked Jerusalem during the reign of King Rehoboam and plundered the Temple and royal palace.

Shoshenq's Palestinian campaign was one of the last significant Egyptian military operations in the Levant. It showed that Egypt could still project power beyond its borders, at least temporarily. However, it didn't restore Egyptian dominance in the region. The campaign was more of a raid than a conquest. Shoshenq took plunder and tribute but didn't establish permanent Egyptian control.

After Shoshenq I's death, the Twenty-second Dynasty continued, but royal authority gradually weakened again. Subsequent pharaohs had less control over the country. Regional strongmen, many of them also of Libyan descent, established local power bases. Governors of major cities became increasingly independent, ruling their territories almost like mini-kingdoms.

By the early 9th century BCE, Egypt was fragmenting again. Multiple rulers claimed royal authority. Historians identify a Twenty-third Dynasty that ruled concurrently with the later Twenty-second Dynasty, based in the delta city of Leontopolis. There was also a Twenty-fourth Dynasty, which briefly ruled from Sais in the western delta. These weren't successive dynasties but overlapping ones. There were different rulers in different cities, all claiming to be pharaoh and all controlling limited territories.

This abundance of pharaohs—sometimes called the "Libyan period" because most of the rulers were of Libyan descent—is confusing even for Egyptologists. The chronology is uncertain, and the relationships between different rulers are unclear. Some pharaohs are known only from a few inscriptions. It's a messy period.

What's clear, though, is that Egypt was weak and divided. No single ruler controlled the entire country. This political fragmentation made Egypt vulnerable. Without a strong central government and a unified military, Egypt couldn't defend itself against external threats. And a major threat was developing to the south—a powerful kingdom that would soon conquer Egypt and briefly reunify the country under foreign rule.

The Nubian Conquest

South of Egypt, in the region called Nubia (roughly corresponding to modern Sudan), a powerful kingdom had emerged. This was the Kingdom of Kush, centered on the city of Napata near the Fourth Cataract of the Nile. The Kushites were culturally connected to Egypt. They worshiped Egyptian gods, particularly Amun, and they saw themselves as inheritors of the Egyptian civilization. However, they were politically independent and becoming increasingly powerful.

Nubia had a long, complex relationship with Egypt. During periods when Egypt was strong, Egypt controlled Nubia, exploiting its gold mines and using it as a source of luxury goods and soldiers. During the New Kingdom, Nubia had been thoroughly Egyptianized, with Egyptian temples, Egyptian administrators, and Egyptian culture imposed on the region.

But when Egypt weakened during the late New Kingdom and the Third Intermediate Period, Nubian independence reasserted itself. A dynasty established itself at Napata. By the 8th century BCE, the Kingdom of Kush had become a major regional power.

The Kushite kings saw themselves as the true upholders of Egyptian tradition and guardians of proper religious practice. While Egypt itself had become fragmented and ruled by Libyan dynasties, the Kushites at Napata maintained Egyptian religious practices with notable devotion. They used Egyptian hieroglyphs and adopted Egyptian royal ideology. In their view, they were preserving authentic Egyptian tradition more faithfully than the rulers in Egypt itself.

Around 760 BCE, a Kushite king named Kashta began expanding northward from Nubia into Upper Egypt. He gained control of Thebes and the surrounding region, establishing Kushite authority over southern Egypt. His daughter Amenirdis became God's Wife of Amun, an important religious position at Thebes.

Kashta's successor, Piye (ruled approximately 747–716 BCE), continued the expansion. Around 728 BCE, Piye launched a major military campaign northward to bring all of Egypt under Kushite control.

An extraordinary document survives from this campaign: the Victory Stela of Piye, a long inscription discovered at Napata. It provides one of the most vivid accounts of ancient Egyptian warfare that has survived from any period.

According to the stela, Piye was motivated by reports that a Delta ruler named Tefnakht, who controlled much of Lower Egypt, was disrespecting the gods and threatening Egyptian tradition. Piye portrayed his campaign as a mission to restore ma'at and proper worship to Egypt.

Piye's army sailed north down the Nile. They encountered resistance from various local rulers (Egypt's political fragmentation meant there were multiple kings and chiefs who had to be defeated individually). The stela describes sieges of cities, naval battles on the Nile, negotiations, and submissions.

When Piye reached Memphis, the city initially resisted. The stela describes how Piye's forces besieged Memphis, attacked its harbor, and eventually captured the city. The victory was celebrated with proper religious rituals. Piye made offerings to the gods and purified the temples that had been "polluted" by improper worship.

The stela lists numerous kings and chiefs who came to bow before the Kushite pharaoh, offering their submission and tribute. Tefnakht himself eventually submitted, though he never personally appeared before Piye. Instead, he sent messages of submission through intermediaries.

Piye's victory stela portrays him as both a mighty warrior and a pious king. He conquered through military force but also through religious authority. He was restoring ma'at and bringing Egypt back to the proper worship of the gods, particularly Amun.

After conquering Egypt, Piye did something unusual—he went home to Nubia. He returned to Napata, leaving Egypt under the control of local rulers who now owed him allegiance. He didn't establish a permanent administrative presence in Egypt or try to rule directly from Memphis or Thebes. He had demonstrated Kushite supremacy and exacted tribute, but he didn't reorganize Egypt's political structure. Perhaps he considered his mission accomplished. After all, Egypt had submitted, proper worship was restored, and his authority was recognized. Perhaps he preferred to rule from Napata, the center of Kushite power. Perhaps he didn't have the resources or interest in permanently occupying Egypt.

Piye's successors took a different approach. His brother Shabaka (ruled approximately 716–702 BCE) actually moved to Egypt and established direct Kushite rule. Shabaka conquered the remaining independent territories in the delta, defeated Tefnakht's successor, and established what historians call the Twenty-fifth Dynasty—the Kushite or Nubian Dynasty.

Shabaka and his successors ruled Egypt from Memphis, presenting themselves as traditional Egyptian pharaohs. They built monuments, restored temples, and patronized Egyptian religion and culture. They commissioned inscriptions in Egyptian hieroglyphs. They also adopted the full Egyptian royal titulary. In many ways, they were model pharaohs, perhaps more devoted to Egyptian tradition than many native Egyptian rulers had been.

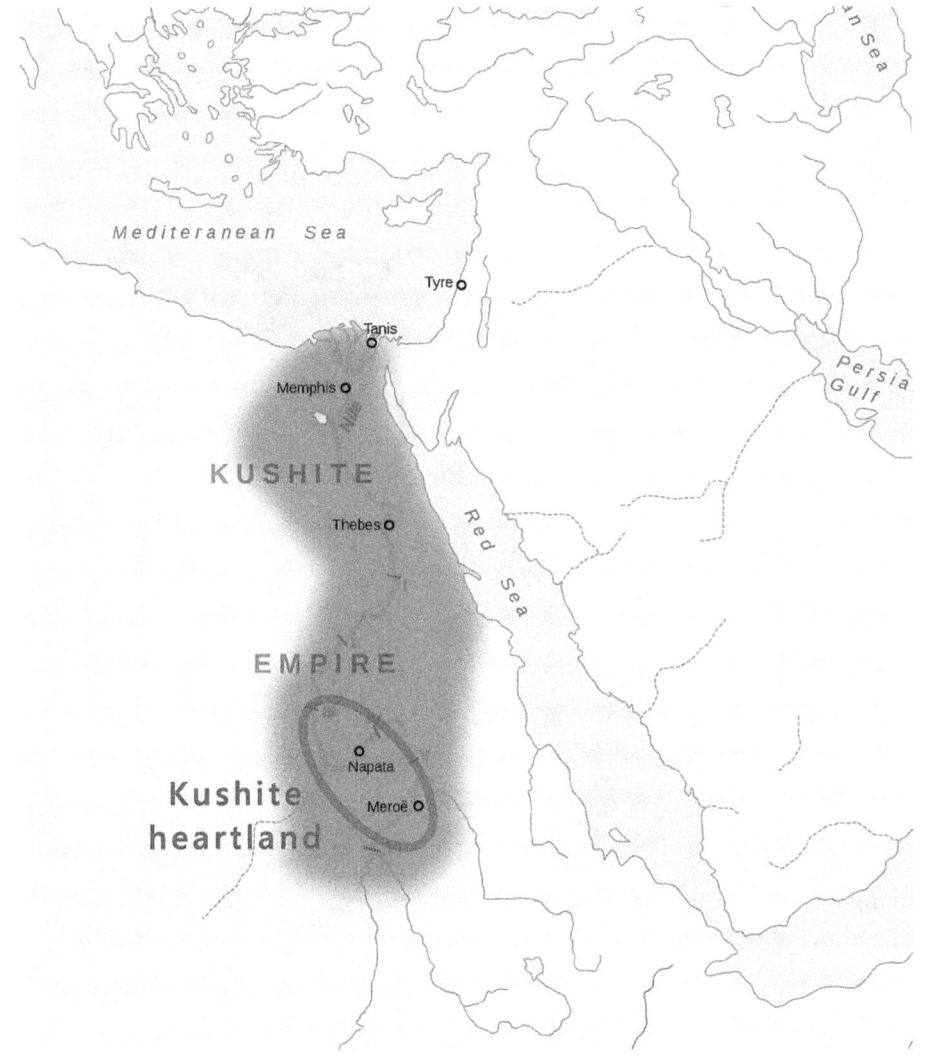

The Kushite Empire around 700 BCE.[54]

The Kushite pharaohs are sometimes called the "Black Pharaohs" in modern literature because they came from a region south of Egypt, which was inhabited by people with darker skin tones than most Egyptians. This is a modern term not used in antiquity, and it's somewhat problematic. Ancient Egyptians didn't categorize people by race in the modern sense, and Nubia had always been part of the Egyptian cultural sphere. But the term reflects the fact that the Twenty-fifth Dynasty represented a period when Egypt was ruled by kings whose base of power was in sub-Saharan Africa.

The most famous Kushite pharaoh was Taharqa (ruled approximately 690–664 BCE), who appears in the Hebrew Bible as King "Tirhakah" of Cush (2 Kings 19:9). Taharqa was an energetic and ambitious ruler. He conducted military campaigns, built extensively throughout Egypt and Nubia, and attempted to restore Egypt to something approaching its former glory.

Taharqa's building program was impressive. He added structures to the Temple of Karnak at Thebes and built temples in Nubia. He restored shrines that had fallen into disrepair during the years of division. Taharqa was trying to rebuild Egypt as a unified, powerful kingdom.

But Taharqa faced a problem that he couldn't overcome—the Assyrian Empire.

The End of Independence

By the 7th century BCE, the Near East was dominated by Assyria, a militaristic empire based in northern Mesopotamia (modern Iraq). The Assyrians had built the most powerful military machine the ancient world had yet seen. They had conquered vast territories, including Mesopotamia, Syria, Palestine, Anatolia, and parts of the Iranian Plateau. They were expanding in all directions, and Egypt was next.

The Assyrian kings wanted to control Egypt for several reasons. Egypt was wealthy. It controlled trade routes

Statue of Tarhaqa.[86]

and had symbolic importance as one of the ancient world's great civilizations. Plus, Egyptian pharaohs had been meddling in the Levant, supporting local rulers who resisted Assyrian domination.

Taharqa, like several Egyptian pharaohs before him, had supported rebellion against Assyria in Palestine. He sent military aid to kingdoms like

Judah when they resisted Assyrian conquest. This was traditional Egyptian foreign policy—supporting buffer states to keep hostile powers away from Egypt's borders. However, it put Egypt directly in conflict with the most powerful empire of the age.

The Assyrian king Esarhaddon (ruled 681–669 BCE) decided to deal with the Egyptian problem decisively. In 674 BCE, he launched an invasion of Egypt. The campaign initially failed. The Assyrian army was defeated, perhaps by environmental factors or Egyptian resistance. But Esarhaddon tried again.

In 671 BCE, Esarhaddon invaded Egypt with a large army. This time, the Assyrians were successful. They defeated Taharqa's forces, captured Memphis, and drove Taharqa south to Thebes. Esarhaddon proclaimed himself "king of Egypt, Kush, and Pathos" and claimed to have conquered the entire country.

The conquest wasn't complete, though. Taharqa still controlled Upper Egypt from Thebes. After Esarhaddon withdrew, Taharqa reoccupied Memphis and reasserted his control over Lower Egypt. The Assyrians had won a battle, but they hadn't secured Egypt.

Esarhaddon died in 669 BCE while preparing another campaign against Egypt. His son Ashurbanipal (ruled 669–631 BCE) continued the war. In 667 BCE, Ashurbanipal led another invasion. Again, the Assyrians captured Memphis, and again, Taharqa retreated to Thebes. This time, the Assyrians pursued farther south, pushing into Upper Egypt.

Taharqa died around 664 BCE, probably in Nubia, where he had retreated after the Assyrian invasions. His successor, Tantamani, briefly attempted to reclaim Egypt, marching north and recapturing Memphis. But Ashurbanipal responded with yet another invasion in 663 BCE. The Assyrians drove Tantamani back to Nubia and decisively sacked Thebes.

This sack of Thebes was devastating. The great city, which had been Egypt's religious capital for over a thousand years, was thoroughly plundered. The Assyrians took vast amounts of gold, silver, and precious objects from Thebes' temples. The sack was so traumatic that it was remembered for generations. The Hebrew prophet Nahum, writing decades later, used the fall of Thebes as an example of how even the mightiest cities could be destroyed (Nahum 3:8–10).

The sack of Thebes marked the end of Kushite rule in Egypt. The Twenty-fifth Dynasty was over. The Nubian pharaohs withdrew to their kingdom in Kush, where they would continue to rule for centuries, building pyramids and maintaining Egyptian cultural traditions. But they never again controlled Egypt itself.

Egypt now came under Assyrian dominance, though this control was exercised indirectly. The Assyrians appointed local Egyptian rulers as vassals, requiring them to pay tribute and maintain loyalty to Assyria. The most important of these vassals was Necho I, ruler of Sais in the western delta, who had sided with the Assyrians against the Kushites.

Necho I and his son Psamtik I (ruled 664–610 BCE) would establish what historians call the Twenty-sixth Dynasty, also known as the Saite Dynasty, after their capital at Sais. This dynasty would eventually restore Egyptian independence and usher in the Late Period of Egyptian history.

In the mid-7th century BCE, Egypt had been invaded by a foreign empire for the first time in its long history. The country that had once dominated the Near East, that had built the pyramids and conquered Syria and Nubia, had seen the great temples of Thebes plundered by foreign soldiers. The Third Intermediate Period—those approximately 350 years of political fragmentation—was ending, but not with a restoration of Egyptian power.

Egypt's cultural traditions remained vibrant and distinctly Egyptian. But the days of Egyptian political dominance were over. The future would bring more foreign rule—Persian, Greek, and eventually Roman—until eventually Egypt became a province in other people's empires.

But Egyptians didn't know that yet. In the aftermath of the Assyrian invasions, there was still hope that Egypt could recover, that the ancient kingdom could restore itself one more time. And surprisingly, that hope wouldn't be entirely disappointed.

Chapter 13: The Late Period—
Twilight and Foreign Shadows

The Saite Renaissance

After the Assyrian invasions drove out the Kushite pharaohs, Egypt seemed finished as an independent power. The great temples of Thebes had been plundered. Foreign armies had marched through the land. Egypt existed under Assyrian overlordship, its rulers reduced to vassals paying tribute to Mesopotamian kings.

But Egypt wasn't done yet. From the city of Sais in the western Nile Delta, a new dynasty would emerge that would restore Egyptian independence and usher in a remarkable cultural revival. The Twenty-sixth Dynasty, also called the Saite Dynasty, would give Egypt one last period of unity, prosperity, and cultural flowering before the final conquest by foreign empires.

The founder of this revival was Psamtik I (ruled 664–610 BCE), though his father Necho I had laid the groundwork. Necho I had been one of the local rulers the Assyrians installed as vassals after defeating the Kushites. He ruled Sais in the Delta and remained loyal to Assyria, even dying in battle against the Kushite pharaoh Tantamani when Tantamani briefly attempted to reclaim Egypt.

When Necho I died, his son Psamtik inherited control of Sais and the Delta region. Psamtik was still nominally an Assyrian vassal, but he had ambitions beyond simply serving as a puppet ruler.

The key to Psamtik's success was timing. By the 650s BCE, Assyria was becoming overextended. The Assyrian Empire had expanded to an enormous size, stretching from Egypt to Mesopotamia to Iran. Managing such a vast territory required constant military campaigns to suppress revolts and maintain control. Assyria was powerful but strained, fighting a massive civil war between rival claimants to the throne and dealing with rebellions throughout its empire, including a major revolt by Babylon.

Psamtik recognized the opportunity. Gradually, carefully, he began asserting independence through diplomatic maneuvering and building alliances, including with Gyges of Lydia in Asia Minor. He didn't openly rebel—that would have brought Assyrian armies down on him. Instead, he stopped paying tribute, ceased acknowledging Assyrian authority, and started expanding his own power within Egypt. Egypt was far away, difficult to reach, and no longer worth the effort required for Assyria to reconquer it.

To accomplish this, Psamtik needed military force. He couldn't rely solely on Egyptian troops—Egypt's military had weakened during the years of division. So Psamtik did something that would become common in the Late Period: he hired foreign mercenaries.

Greek mercenaries from Ionia and Caria in Asia Minor came to Egypt in large numbers during Psamtik's reign. These Greeks were professional soldiers, well-trained and equipped. Psamtik also employed Carian mercenaries and other foreigners. He established these mercenaries in military colonies in Egypt, particularly in the delta, giving them land in exchange for military service.

With his mercenary army, Psamtik gradually brought all of Egypt under his control, though this required some limited military action against rival Delta rulers and the assertion of authority through military presence in Upper Egypt. He expanded from his base in Sais to control the entire Nile Delta. He moved south, asserting authority over Middle Egypt. The crucial moment came when he gained control of Thebes and Upper Egypt.

The High Priests of Amun at Thebes had ruled southern Egypt independently for generations. To secure their cooperation, Psamtik used a clever strategy. There was a religious position at Thebes called "God's Wife of Amun"—a priestess who held enormous religious and economic power, which carried significant political influence. The position was typically held by a royal princess who remained celibate, and upon her death, another royal princess would be adopted as her successor.

Psamtik arranged for his daughter Nitocris to be adopted by the current God's Wife of Amun as her successor. This gave Psamtik's family control over Thebes' religious establishment and its vast economic resources, and through this religious and economic authority, effective political influence over Upper Egypt. When Nitocris eventually became God's Wife of Amun, she wielded considerable power in southern Egypt on behalf of her father and later her brother.

By around 656 BCE, just eight years after becoming ruler of Sais, Psamtik controlled all of Egypt. He had reunified the country without major warfare, through a combination of military force, political maneuvering, and religious diplomacy. Egypt was independent again, free from Assyrian control.

Psamtik I ruled for 54 years, making his one of the longest reigns in Egyptian history, though not quite matching the extraordinary lengths of Ramesses II (66 years) or Pepi II (possibly 64-94 years). His reign was largely peaceful and prosperous. He didn't conduct major military campaigns abroad—Egypt's days of empire-building were over. But he stabilized Egypt internally, promoted trade, and presided over a cultural renaissance.

This cultural revival is what makes the Saite Period so interesting. Psamtik and his successors deliberately looked backward to Egypt's glorious past, particularly to the Old Kingdom and Middle Kingdom, seeking to recapture the artistic styles and cultural achievements of those earlier periods.

Saite art is characterized by this archaism—the deliberate imitation of earlier styles. Sculptors studied Old Kingdom statues and created new works in the same style. Hieroglyphic inscriptions used archaic forms of language. Religious texts revived ancient spells and rituals that had fallen out of use. Tomb designs imitated earlier periods.

This wasn't simple nostalgia. It was a deliberate political and cultural statement. By connecting themselves to Egypt's ancient past, the Saite pharaohs were asserting continuity with the great pharaohs of old. They were saying: we are the legitimate successors to the pyramid builders, to the great conquerors, to the traditional Egyptian kings. The years of division and foreign rule were an aberration; we have restored the true Egypt.

The Saite Period also saw increased contact with the Greek world. The Greek mercenaries Psamtik had hired remained in Egypt, establishing communities. Greek traders came to Egypt in large numbers, establishing a major trading post at Naucratis in the delta, which became the primary port for Greek commerce with Egypt.

This Greek presence would have enormous long-term consequences. Greeks were fascinated by Egypt—its ancient civilization, its mysterious religion, its monumental architecture. Greek historians like Herodotus would visit Egypt and write about it, spreading knowledge of Egyptian civilization throughout the Mediterranean world. This Greek interest in Egypt would eventually lead to the Greek conquest of Egypt under Alexander the Great, but that was still centuries away.

Psamtik's successors continued his policies. His son Necho II (ruled 610-595 BCE) was more militarily ambitious. He attempted to expand Egyptian power into Palestine. The Assyrian Empire was falling apart in the late 7th century BCE, as it was being destroyed by a coalition of Babylonians, Medes, and others. Necho II saw an opportunity to reclaim some of Egypt's old territories in the Levant.

In 609 BCE, Necho II marched north with an Egyptian army, intending to support what remained of Assyria against the Babylonians. This was not because he liked the Assyrians but because he didn't want Babylon to become too powerful. On his way north, he encountered the army of King Josiah of Judah at Megiddo. Josiah, who was allied with Babylon, tried to stop the Egyptian army. The battle was brief. Josiah was killed, and Necho's army continued north.

Necho briefly controlled parts of Syria-Palestine, but his control didn't last. In 605 BCE, the Babylonian crown prince Nebuchadnezzar (yes, the same Nebuchadnezzar who would later destroy Jerusalem) defeated Necho's army at the Battle of Carchemish in Syria. The Egyptians were driven back, and Babylon, not Egypt, became the dominant power in the Levant.

Necho II is also famous for allegedly attempting to circumnavigate Africa. According to the Greek historian Herodotus, Necho hired Phoenician sailors to sail around Africa, starting from the Red Sea and returning via the Mediterranean. The expedition supposedly took three years and succeeded in completing the journey. Modern historians debate whether this actually happened—Herodotus himself expressed skepticism about some details—but it's possible that such an expedition occurred.

Later Saite pharaohs—Psamtik II, Apries, and Amasis—continued to rule Egypt with varying degrees of success. The Saite Dynasty maintained

Egypt's traditional culture while also engaging with the wider Mediterranean world. Greek mercenaries and traders became an increasingly important part of Egyptian society. Egypt was no longer isolated but was becoming integrated into the broader Mediterranean commercial and cultural network.

The last significant Saite pharaoh was Amasis (ruled 570-526 BCE), who came to power through a military coup but proved to be an effective ruler. He maintained good relations with the Greek world, married a Greek woman from Cyrene, and promoted trade with Greece. Under Amasis, Egypt experienced prosperity and stability.

But the Saite revival was about to come to an abrupt end. A new power was rising in the east—Persia—and Egypt was directly in its path. In the mid-6th century BCE, the world's geopolitical landscape changed dramatically. The Persian Empire, under its founder Cyrus the Great, exploded onto the scene, conquering territory at an astonishing rate. Within a few decades, Persia had conquered Media, Lydia, Babylonia, and much of the Near East and central Asia, creating the largest empire the world had yet seen.

Egypt watched nervously. The Persians were clearly building toward a conquest of Egypt. It was the last major independent kingdom in the region, and controlling Egypt would give Persia access to Egypt's wealth and complete Persian domination of the eastern Mediterranean.

Amasis, the Saite pharaoh, tried to prepare. He made alliances with Greek city-states and strengthened Egypt's defenses. He also hired more Greek mercenaries. However, in 526 BCE, before the Persian invasion came, Amasis died. His son Psamtik III became pharaoh, inheriting a kingdom under threat.

In 525 BCE, the Persian king Cambyses II invaded Egypt with a large army. The Egyptians met the Persians at Pelusium, a fortress city in the eastern delta that guarded the approach to Egypt from the Levant. The Battle of Pelusium was decisive. The Persian army, experienced from decades of conquests, defeated the Egyptian forces.

The Persians then marched on Memphis. Psamtik III retreated to the capital, but Memphis quickly fell. Psamtik was captured. According to the Greek historian Herodotus, Cambyses initially spared him but later had him executed when Psamtik allegedly tried to organize a revolt. Whether this story is true or not, Psamtik disappears from the records. The Saite Dynasty was over. Egypt became part of the Persian Empire.

Cambyses's conquest started the Twenty-seventh Dynasty. Egyptians didn't recognize it as a legitimate dynasty, though. To them, the Persians were foreign conquerors, not true pharaohs.

The Persians ruled Egypt as a satrapy—a province of their empire governed by a Persian-appointed satrap (governor). The satrap collected taxes, maintained order, and ensured Egypt's loyalty to the Persian king. However, the Persians often appointed Egyptians to many high administrative positions within the satrapy, recognizing the importance of local expertise and cooperation.

The Persians were practical. They realized that Egypt had a proud, ancient culture and that ruling Egypt required respecting, or at least accommodating, Egyptian traditions. Persian kings took Egyptian royal titles and presented themselves as pharaohs, at least in official Egyptian documents. They made offerings to Egyptian gods and respected Egyptian temples and priesthoods.

Cambyses's reputation in later Egyptian tradition is terrible. Egyptian sources portray him as a monster who killed the sacred Apis bull, desecrated temples, and mocked Egyptian religion. According to these accounts, he went mad and died as divine punishment for his sacrilege.

How much of this is true? Probably very little. These stories come from sources written much later, during periods when Egypt was trying to resist Persian rule. They're propaganda designed to delegitimize Persian authority. The stories of his madness and sacrilege are likely inventions.

But even if the Persian kings weren't the monsters later tradition made them out to be, Persian rule was unpopular in Egypt. The Egyptians had enjoyed independence under the Saite Dynasty. They didn't like being ruled by foreigners, even relatively respectful ones. Throughout the Persian period, Egyptians would repeatedly revolt, attempting to regain independence.

The second Persian king to rule Egypt, Darius I (ruled 522–486 BCE), was more systematic in his approach. He commissioned the recording and clarification of existing Egyptian laws, completed a canal connecting the Nile to the Red Sea (begun earlier under the Saite pharaohs), and generally tried to integrate Egypt into the Persian administrative system while maintaining the accommodations to Egyptian traditions that had been established. However, he was also extracting significant tribute from Egypt to fund Persian military campaigns elsewhere in the empire.

The Persian period also coincided with major geopolitical changes in the Mediterranean. The Greeks and Persians fought a series of wars, such as the famous Greco-Persian Wars. Egypt, as a Persian province, was drawn into these conflicts. According to Herodotus, Egyptians fought in Persian naval operations against the Greeks, and Egyptian resources supported Persian military campaigns.

In 486 BCE, when Darius I died and his son Xerxes I became king, Egypt revolted. The timing seemed perfect—Xerxes was preoccupied with preparations for his massive invasion of Greece. But Xerxes dealt with the Egyptian revolt swiftly, sending an army that suppressed the rebellion before he launched his Greek campaign.

After the Persian defeat in Greece, Persian control over Egypt weakened. In 460 BCE, a major Egyptian revolt broke out, led by a Libyan prince named Inaros. The rebels controlled much of the delta and even besieged Persian forces in Memphis.

The Athenians, who were at war with Persia, sent a fleet to support the Egyptian rebels. For several years, the Egyptians and their Athenian allies fought Persian forces in Egypt. The rebellion initially succeeded. Inaros defeated a Persian army and controlled significant Egyptian territory.

But Persia was vast and powerful. It assembled a huge army and sent it to Egypt. In 454 BCE, the Persian army crushed the rebellion. Inaros was captured and eventually executed. The Athenian fleet was destroyed. Egypt was firmly under Persian control again.

Another major revolt occurred in 404 BCE, at the very end of Darius II's reign. This time, the revolt succeeded. A native Egyptian named Amyrtaeus, ruling from Sais in the delta, led a successful rebellion and expelled the Persians from Egypt. Egypt was independent again.

Amyrtaeus established the Twenty-eighth Dynasty, but his reign was brief—only about six years. He was overthrown and killed by Nepherites I, who founded the Twenty-ninth Dynasty, ruling from Mendes in the delta.

The Twenty-ninth and Thirtieth Dynasties (collectively 404–343 BCE) represent the last period of native Egyptian rule. These dynasties, ruling from various delta cities, maintained Egyptian independence for about sixty years, successfully resisting several Persian attempts to reconquer Egypt.

These native Egyptian pharaohs were constantly preparing for a Persian invasion. They hired Greek mercenaries in large numbers. They built fortifications and made alliances with Greek city-states, particularly Sparta and Athens, which were happy to support anyone fighting against Persia.

The last native Egyptian dynasty, the Thirtieth, was the most successful. Its pharaohs, particularly Nectanebo I and Nectanebo II, successfully defended Egypt against multiple Persian invasions. They built extensively, including major additions to temples throughout Egypt. They promoted Egyptian culture and religion. For a brief moment, it seemed Egypt might maintain its independence.

But Persia was regrouping. Under Artaxerxes III, a powerful and ruthless king, Persia reconquered much of its lost territory. In 343 BCE, Artaxerxes launched a massive invasion of Egypt with an enormous army—ancient sources claim hundreds of thousands of troops, though these numbers are clearly exaggerated, as was typical in ancient accounts.

Nectanebo II, the last native Egyptian pharaoh, tried to resist. He had fortified the delta. He had hired thousands of Greek mercenaries. He had prepared for years for this invasion.

The head of Nectanebo II.[56]

But the Persian army was too strong. It broke through Egypt's defenses, defeated the Egyptian army, and marched on Memphis. Nectanebo II fled south, eventually escaping to Nubia. Egypt fell to Persia again.

The Thirty-first Dynasty in Egyptian chronology was remembered by later Egyptian sources as particularly harsh. According to these accounts, Artaxerxes III plundered temples, confiscated the temples' wealth, and treated Egypt more as a conquered territory than as a satrapy deserving respect. Archaeological evidence for the severity of this treatment varies by region.

Egypt would remain under Persian control for only about a decade. But for Egyptians, that decade must have seemed hopeless. The last native pharaoh had fled. The temples were plundered. Foreign troops occupied Egypt. The long tradition of native Egyptian pharaonic rule appeared to be ending.

But history had one more surprise in store. A young Macedonian king named Alexander was about to change the world, and Egypt would be transformed yet again.

Chapter 14:
Alexander, Ptolemies, and the End

Alexander the Great

In 332 BCE, a twenty-four-year-old Macedonian king arrived in Egypt and changed its history forever. Alexander III of Macedon—known to history as Alexander the Great—had already accomplished what seemed impossible: he had defeated the mighty Persian Empire in a series of brilliant military campaigns. Now he was bringing his army to Egypt, the richest province in the Persian realm.

After a decade of harsh Persian rule, Egyptians were eager to be free of their conquerors. When Alexander's army approached Egypt from Palestine, the Persian satrap Mazaces surrendered Egypt without a fight. Alexander entered Egypt peacefully, welcomed as a liberator.

Alexander understood the importance of respecting Egyptian culture and religion. He presented himself as a legitimate pharaoh in official Egyptian contexts, not as a foreign invader. He made the proper offerings to Egyptian gods. He adopted Egyptian royal titles and presented himself as the successor to the ancient pharaohs.

This wasn't just political calculation, though it was certainly that. Alexander seemed interested in Egyptian traditions, though how much was genuine curiosity versus political strategy remains debated by historians. He was educated by the philosopher Aristotle and had been raised on Greek culture, which already held Egypt in high regard as an ancient land of wisdom and mystery. The Greeks had been trading with and learning from Egypt for centuries. For Alexander, Egypt represented something ancient, sacred, and worthy of respect.

One of Alexander's first major acts in Egypt was to make a pilgrimage to the oracle of Amun at the Siwa Oasis in the western desert. This was a famous oracle that the Greeks identified with their own god, Zeus. Alexander traveled across hundreds of miles of desert to reach Siwa, where the priests of Amun greeted him.

What happened at Siwa remains unknown. Greek accounts report that the oracle addressed Alexander in a way that was interpreted as recognizing him as the son of Zeus-Amun, confirming his divine status. In Egyptian terms, this meant the god Amun acknowledged Alexander as pharaoh—the god's earthly representative. Whether Alexander actually believed he was divine or whether this was political theater is debated. But the visit to Siwa gave Alexander religious legitimacy in Egyptian eyes and reinforced his position as Egypt's rightful ruler.

Alexander's most lasting contribution to Egypt was the founding of Alexandria. On the Mediterranean coast, on a strip of land between the sea and Lake Mareotis, Alexander chose a site for a new city. According to later tradition, he personally laid out the city's plan, marking the streets with barley meal since chalk wasn't available. The actual architect was likely Dinocrates of Rhodes. He envisioned a great city that would be a center of commerce and culture, connecting Egypt to the Mediterranean world.

Alexandria would become one of the greatest cities of the ancient world, but Alexander wouldn't live to see it. He spent only about six months in Egypt before leaving to continue his conquest of the Persian Empire. He marched east, eventually reaching as far as India. He never returned to Egypt.

In 323 BCE, at the age of thirty-two, Alexander died in Babylon. Modern scholars generally agree that illness—possibly typhoid fever or malaria—was the most likely cause, though ancient sources speculated about poisoning and other theories. His death threw his vast empire into chaos. He had conquered everything from Greece to India, but he had no clear heir. His son would be born after his death, and the child would never rule. Instead, Alexander's generals would fight over his empire for decades.

One of these generals was Ptolemy, who had been one of Alexander's closest companions and most trusted commanders. When Alexander's generals began dividing up the empire, Ptolemy moved quickly to seize Egypt. He understood that Egypt, with its wealth, natural defenses, and ancient prestige, was the most valuable prize.

Ptolemy also did something symbolically important: he diverted Alexander's funeral procession. Alexander's body was being transported from Babylon to Macedonia for burial, but Ptolemy intercepted it and brought it to Egypt instead. By controlling Alexander's body and tomb, Ptolemy was claiming to be Alexander's legitimate successor, at least in Egypt.

The Ptolemaic Dynasty

Ptolemy initially ruled Egypt as satrap, nominally governing on behalf of Alexander's infant son and mentally impaired half-brother, who were the technical heirs to Alexander's empire. But as the wars among Alexander's successors dragged on and it became clear that no one would reunify the empire, Ptolemy declared himself king around 305 BCE. He became Ptolemy I Soter ("Savior"), founder of the Ptolemaic dynasty, which would rule Egypt for nearly three centuries.

The Ptolemaic dynasty was Greek. The Ptolemies spoke Greek, promoted Greek culture, and surrounded themselves with Greek courtiers and officials. Alexandria became a Greek city, the capital of a Greek-ruled kingdom. The Ptolemies brought thousands of Greek and Macedonian settlers to Egypt, establishing Greek colonies and creating a Greek-speaking ruling class.

However, the Ptolemies also understood that to rule Egypt effectively, they needed to accommodate Egyptian traditions. This created a dual system. To the Greeks living in Alexandria and the Greek cities of Egypt, the Ptolemies were Greek kings ruling a Hellenistic kingdom. To the native Egyptians living in the countryside and worshiping in ancient temples, the Ptolemies were pharaohs, the latest in a line stretching back millennia. The same ruler presented two different faces depending on the audience. They commissioned temples built in the traditional Egyptian style, made offerings to Egyptian gods, had themselves depicted in Egyptian art wearing traditional pharaonic regalia, took Egyptian royal titles, and participated in Egyptian religious ceremonies.

The early Ptolemaic period was Egypt's last great age of prosperity. Ptolemy I and his successors rebuilt Alexandria into one of the Mediterranean's most magnificent cities. The city featured wide streets laid out in a grid pattern, impressive public buildings, royal palaces, and harbors. It was the commercial hub of the eastern Mediterranean.

Most famously, the Ptolemies built the Library of Alexandria, which became the ancient world's greatest center of learning. The library aimed to collect all the knowledge in the world, and at its height, it possibly contained hundreds of thousands of scrolls. Scholars from throughout the Mediterranean came to Alexandria to study. The library housed works of literature, philosophy, science, mathematics, and medicine. It was a research center where scholars translated texts, wrote commentaries, and conducted investigations.

The library was part of a larger institution called the Mouseion (Museum)—literally a "temple to the Muses"—which functioned like a modern university and research institute. Scholars at the Mouseion received royal patronage to pursue their studies. They gave lectures, conducted experiments, engaged in philosophical debates, and produced scholarly works.

Some of the ancient world's greatest intellectuals worked in Alexandria during the Ptolemaic period. Euclid wrote his geometry textbook there. Eratosthenes calculated the Earth's circumference with remarkable accuracy. The physician Herophilus conducted anatomical studies. The poet Callimachus catalogued the library's holdings. Alexandria became the intellectual capital of the ancient world, attracting brilliant minds and producing groundbreaking scholarship.

The Ptolemies also built the Pharos of Alexandria, one of the Seven Wonders of the Ancient World. This massive lighthouse, standing over 330 feet tall on an island in Alexandria's harbor, guided ships safely to port with a light that could reportedly be seen for many miles. The Pharos became so famous that its name became the word for lighthouse in several languages (like *faro* in Spanish and Italian).

A 1572 depiction of the Lighthouse of Alexandria—the earliest known representation of it in modern times.[87]

But beneath this cultural brilliance, the Ptolemaic kingdom had serious problems. The dynasty was plagued by internal conflict. Ptolemaic kings and queens fought each other for power in brutal civil wars. Family members murdered each other. Siblings married each other (the Ptolemies adopted the Egyptian royal practice of brother-sister marriage, which they took to extremes).

The Ptolemies also faced resistance from native Egyptians. While they presented themselves as pharaohs and respected the Egyptian religion, they were still foreign rulers whose primary interest was extracting wealth from Egypt to support their wars and lavish lifestyles. The Greek population lived largely separate from native Egyptians, creating social and cultural divisions. Native Egyptians mounted major revolts, particularly in Upper Egypt, where Egyptian culture remained strongest. Some of these rebellions were massive, occasionally leading to periods of de facto native rule in the south.

The dynasty's wealth came largely from agriculture. Egypt's incredibly fertile soil, watered by the Nile's annual floods, produced enormous grain harvests. The Ptolemies exported grain throughout the Mediterranean, making Egypt a major grain supplier for the ancient world. They also controlled trade routes connecting the Mediterranean to the Red Sea, Arabia, and India, profiting from the spice trade and luxury goods.

However, running this economic system required a massive bureaucracy. The Ptolemies created an elaborate administrative apparatus that controlled virtually every aspect of Egyptian economic life. They taxed everything—agricultural production, trade, manufacturing, even activities like fishing and beekeeping. The bureaucracy kept detailed records in Greek, recording taxes, land ownership, production quotas, and administrative decisions. Egypt under the Ptolemies was one of the most thoroughly documented and bureaucratized states in the ancient world.

As the Ptolemaic period continued, the dynasty gradually weakened. Later Ptolemies were less capable than the early kings. Court intrigues intensified. Civil wars became more frequent and destructive. Egypt's economy suffered. Native Egyptian revolts became more serious and harder to suppress.

And a new power was rising in the west—Rome.

Rome had conquered Italy, then defeated Carthage, and then expanded throughout the Mediterranean. By the 2nd century BCE, Rome was the dominant power in the Mediterranean world. The Ptolemies, recognizing Rome's strength, tried to maintain good relations, even declaring Rome as Egypt's protector in their wills. But this made Egypt increasingly dependent on Rome and vulnerable to Roman interference.

By the 1st century BCE, the Ptolemaic dynasty was clearly in decline. Egypt remained wealthy, but the royal family was dysfunctional, the government was corrupt, and Roman influence was growing. The last great Ptolemaic ruler was a woman who became one of history's most famous figures—Cleopatra VII.

Cleopatra: The Last Pharaoh

When most people hear the name Cleopatra, they think of seduction, romance, and beauty. Hollywood movies have depicted her as the ultimate femme fatale, using her charms to manipulate powerful Roman men. This popular image isn't entirely wrong—Cleopatra did have relationships with Julius Caesar and Mark Antony—but it's incomplete and misleading.

Cleopatra and Caesar by Jean-Léon Gérôme (1866).⁸⁸

Cleopatra VII was born in 69 BCE. She was the daughter of Ptolemy XII, a weak and unpopular king who spent much of his reign trying to maintain his throne with Roman support. When Ptolemy XII died in 51 BCE, Cleopatra inherited the throne with her younger brother, Ptolemy XIII, whom she was required to marry under Ptolemaic custom. She was eighteen years old; he was about ten.

Cleopatra quickly showed that she was more capable and ambitious than her brother. She took control of the government and ruled effectively, even dropping her brother's name from official documents—a serious violation of protocol. This created conflict with powerful courtiers who supported Ptolemy XIII. By 48 BCE, Cleopatra had been driven out of Alexandria by her brother's supporters and was raising an army to reclaim her throne.

At this point, Julius Caesar arrived in Egypt.

Caesar was pursuing his rival Pompey, with whom he was fighting a civil war for control of Rome. Pompey fled to Egypt seeking refuge, but Ptolemy XIII's advisors, hoping to curry favor with Caesar, had Pompey murdered. When Caesar arrived in Alexandria, they presented him with Pompey's severed head.

Caesar was reportedly horrified. Pompey had been his enemy, but he was also a fellow high-ranking Roman. Murdering him was dishonorable. Caesar also saw an opportunity. Egypt was wealthy and strategically important. The Ptolemaic civil war gave him an excuse to intervene.

According to Roman tradition, Cleopatra had herself smuggled into Caesar's presence wrapped in a carpet (or possibly a laundry bag). This dramatic entrance caught Caesar's attention. The two quickly formed an alliance. It was certainly political, but it was also apparently romantic and personal.

Caesar supported Cleopatra against her brother. The conflict escalated into the Alexandrian War, during which parts of Alexandria were burned. Some sources state that parts of the Great Library or storage facilities were damaged during this conflict, though the extent of any damage is debated; most scholars believe the main Great Library survived this event. Ptolemy XIII drowned in the Nile while trying to escape. Caesar installed Cleopatra as Egypt's ruler, along with her younger brother Ptolemy XIV (whom she also married as co-ruler, though he was only about twelve years old and had no real power).

Cleopatra and Caesar also had a son, Caesarion ("Little Caesar"), whom Cleopatra claimed was Caesar's heir. Caesar never officially acknowledged him, but he apparently accepted paternity privately. Cleopatra visited Rome with Caesarion and lived in one of Caesar's villas, which scandalized Roman society. A foreign queen living openly in Rome was shocking to Roman sensibilities.

In 44 BCE, Caesar was assassinated in Rome. Cleopatra fled back to Egypt. Her brother-husband Ptolemy XIV died shortly after (possibly poisoned on her orders), and Cleopatra made her son Caesarion co-ruler.

Egypt and Rome were now interconnected. Rome's civil wars would determine Egypt's fate. After Caesar's death, his assassins were defeated by his supporters, primarily Mark Antony and Octavian (Caesar's adopted heir). Antony and Octavian then divided the Roman world between them, with Antony controlling the eastern Mediterranean.

In 41 BCE, Antony summoned Cleopatra to meet him in Tarsus (in modern Turkey). He wanted Egyptian financial support for his planned military campaigns against Parthia. Cleopatra arrived in spectacular fashion, sailing up the river in an elaborate gilded barge, dressed as the goddess Venus/Aphrodite, demonstrating Egypt's wealth and her own elegance.

Antony and Cleopatra formed both a political alliance and a personal relationship. They had three children together. Antony spent extended periods in Alexandria with Cleopatra. They lived lavishly, throwing elaborate parties and enjoying Egypt's wealth. Roman propaganda portrayed Antony as having "gone native," abandoning Roman values for Eastern luxury and being controlled by a foreign queen.

Politically, the alliance made sense for both of them. Cleopatra needed Roman military protection. Antony needed Egyptian wealth to fund his armies. Together, they formed a powerful bloc in the eastern Mediterranean.

But this partnership threatened Octavian, who controlled the western Mediterranean. Octavian portrayed himself as defending traditional Roman values against the corruption of the East. He waged a propaganda campaign against Antony and Cleopatra, depicting Antony as a traitor who had abandoned Rome for Egypt and was planning to make Cleopatra queen of the Roman Empire with Alexandria as the capital.

In 32 BCE, the Roman Senate, dominated by Octavian's supporters, declared war on Cleopatra (not on Antony, though he was their real target). The conflict came to a head at the Battle of Actium in 31 BCE.

Actium was a naval battle fought off the western coast of Greece. Antony and Cleopatra's fleet faced Octavian's fleet. The battle didn't go well for Antony and Cleopatra. Ancient sources disagree on the details, but at some point during the battle, Cleopatra's ships broke away and fled. Antony followed her. Their fleet was defeated, and their army surrendered.

Why did Cleopatra flee? Ancient sources, mostly hostile to her, claim she panicked or betrayed Antony. Modern historians suggest she might have realized the battle was lost and tried to preserve her forces for continued resistance. Whatever the reason, Actium was a decisive defeat.

Antony and Cleopatra retreated to Alexandria. Octavian pursued them, invading Egypt in 30 BCE. As Octavian's forces approached Alexandria, Antony and Cleopatra's situation became hopeless. Their allies deserted them, and their troops surrendered. Egypt was lost.

According to ancient accounts, Cleopatra retreated to her mausoleum (a tomb she had been building). Antony, receiving a false report that Cleopatra had died, attempted suicide by falling on his sword. Mortally wounded, he was brought to Cleopatra's mausoleum, where he died in her arms.

Cleopatra was captured by Octavian's forces. Octavian wanted to take her back to Rome to display in his triumph—a humiliating public parade celebrating his victory. Cleopatra, determined not to be paraded through Rome as a captive, committed suicide. According to tradition, she died from the bite of an asp (an Egyptian cobra), though the exact method is uncertain. She was thirty-nine years old.

Death of Cleopatra by Jean-Baptiste Regnault (1796–1797).[89]

Octavian had Caesarion killed, eliminating any potential rival who could claim to be Caesar's heir. Cleopatra's children with Antony were taken to Rome and raised by Antony's Roman wife.

With Cleopatra's death, the Ptolemaic dynasty ended. Egypt became a Roman province. It would remain under Roman control, and later Byzantine control, for centuries. The age of the pharaohs was over.

Cleopatra was far more than the seductress of popular imagination. She was the only Ptolemaic ruler who learned to speak Egyptian (the other Ptolemies spoke only Greek). Ancient sources report that she spoke multiple languages—perhaps eight or nine—and could converse with diplomats from throughout the known world without translators. She was educated in philosophy, mathematics, astronomy, and literature. She was a capable administrator who managed Egypt's complex economy. Cleopatra was a political strategist who fought desperately to preserve Egyptian independence, pursuing every possible strategy against overwhelming odds.

That she ultimately failed was perhaps inevitable. Rome was too powerful, building an empire that would eventually control the entire Mediterranean world. After Cleopatra, Egyptian culture would continue and evolve, and Roman emperors would even be recognized as pharaohs in Egyptian temple inscriptions for centuries. However, the long tradition of independent Egyptian or Hellenistic pharaonic rule died with her in 30 BCE.

A Roman sculpture of Cleopatra.[40]

Chapter 15:
Religion and the Afterlife

The Egyptian Pantheon

Before we close out the book, let's take a deeper dive into ancient Egyptian culture. We'll start with religion. Ancient Egyptian religion was complex, fluid, and sometimes confusing even to modern scholars who have spent careers studying it. Unlike monotheistic religions with a single god and clear theological doctrines, Egyptian religion featured hundreds of gods and goddesses, no single authoritative scripture, and beliefs that evolved and changed over three thousand years. Gods could merge with each other, take different forms, and be worshiped differently in different places. Yet for all its complexity, Egyptian religion shaped virtually every aspect of Egyptian life.

The Egyptians didn't have a single word equivalent to "religion." Religious practice, ritual, and belief were simply woven into the fabric of existence. The gods were real, present forces that needed to be honored and appeased. Ma'at—the principle of truth, justice, order, and cosmic balance—had to be maintained through proper worship and ritual. The pharaoh served as the intermediary between humans and gods, maintaining ma'at through his performance of religious duties.

The Egyptian pantheon included dozens of major gods and hundreds of minor ones. Some gods were worshiped throughout Egypt, while others were local deities important only in specific regions. Some gods had clear roles and associations, while others had overlapping or contradictory functions. Gods could be depicted in human form, animal form, or hybrid forms combining human and animal features.

Ra (also called Re) was the sun god. He was one of the most important deities in Egyptian religion. He represented the sun's power and its daily journey across the sky. Egyptians believed Ra traveled through the underworld each night, battling the forces of chaos before being reborn each dawn. Ra was often depicted as a man with a falcon head topped by a sun disk. He became so important that many other gods merged with him, creating composite deities like Amun-Ra.

Osiris was the god of the dead and the afterlife, making him one of Egypt's most important and beloved deities. According to Egyptian mythology, Osiris had once been a king of Egypt who taught humans agriculture and civilization. His brother Seth, jealous of Osiris's power, murdered him. In some versions of the myth, particularly those preserved in later Greek retellings, Seth dismembered Osiris's body and scattered the pieces throughout Egypt. Osiris's wife, Isis, searched for the pieces, reassembled his body, and through magic temporarily restored him to life long enough to conceive a son, Horus. Osiris then became the ruler of the underworld, judging the dead and determining who could enter the afterlife. He was typically depicted as a mummified king, painted green or black, holding the symbols of kingship.

Isis was one of the most popular and powerful goddesses. She was associated with magic, motherhood, and protection. Her devotion to Osiris and her role in raising their son Horus made her a model of loyalty and maternal love. She was worshiped throughout Egypt, and her cult eventually spread throughout the Mediterranean world, with temples to Isis built as far away as Britain. She was typically depicted as a woman wearing a throne-shaped headdress or with cow horns and a sun disk.

Horus, the son of Osiris and Isis, was a sky god closely associated with kingship. The reigning pharaoh was considered a living manifestation of Horus. According to mythology, Horus fought his uncle Seth to avenge his father's murder and reclaim the throne of Egypt. After a long conflict, Horus was declared the rightful king. Horus was most commonly depicted as a falcon or as a man with a falcon head. The famous Eye of Horus symbol—representing wholeness, healing, and protection—was one of ancient Egypt's most common protective amulets.

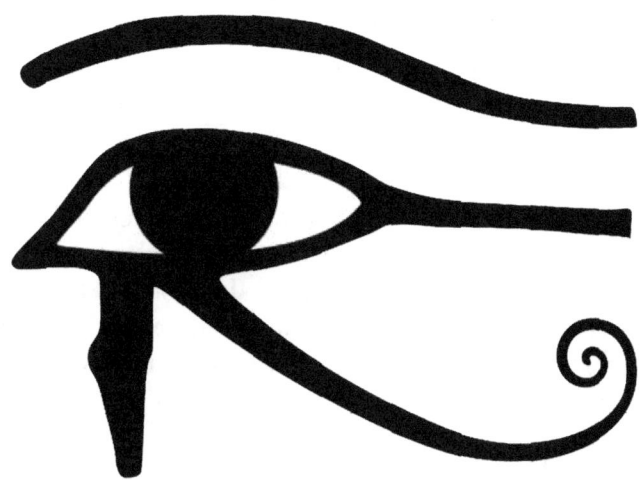

The Eye of Horus.[41]

Anubis was the god of embalming and the protector of the dead. He guided souls through the underworld and oversaw the mummification process. He was typically depicted as a black jackal or as a man with a jackal's head. Black represented both the color of mummified flesh and the fertile black soil of Egypt, symbolizing rebirth.

Thoth was the god of writing, knowledge, magic, and the moon. He was credited with inventing hieroglyphics and served as the scribe of the gods. He was depicted either as an ibis-headed man or as a baboon. Thoth played an important role in the judgment of the dead, recording the results when the deceased's heart was weighed against the feather of ma'at (more on this later).

Seth (also called Set) was the god of chaos, storms, and the desert. He was the murderer of Osiris and the enemy of Horus, yet he also protected Ra's solar boat during its nightly journey through the underworld, fighting off the serpent of chaos, Apophis. Seth represented necessary chaos and wild power. He was dangerous but sometimes useful. He was depicted as a mysterious animal called the "Seth animal," which doesn't correspond to any known creature, with a curved snout, squared ears, and a forked tail.

Hathor was the goddess of love, beauty, music, and joy. She was often depicted as a cow or as a woman with cow ears and horns. She was associated with motherhood, fertility, and celebration. Hathor was also connected to the sky and was sometimes identified as the mother or wife of Horus.

Ptah was the creator god worshiped at Memphis, the patron of craftsmen and architects. Unlike other creator gods who made the world through physical means, Ptah created through thought and speech. He conceived of creation in his heart and brought it into being through his words. He was typically depicted as a mummified man.

Amun was originally a local Theban god who rose to supreme importance during the New Kingdom when Thebes became Egypt's capital. He was associated with air, wind, and hidden power. He merged with Ra to become Amun-Ra, king of the gods. The Amun temple complex at Karnak became the wealthiest and most powerful religious institution in Egypt. Amun was depicted as a man wearing a crown with two tall plumes.

THE DISROBING OF AMEN-RÊ

Amun depicted with Seti I.[43]

This is just a small sampling—there were hundreds more gods and goddesses, including Bastet (cat goddess of home and protection), Sekhmet (lioness goddess of war and healing), Sobek (crocodile god of the Nile), Bes (dwarf god who protected households and children), and Taweret (hippopotamus goddess of childbirth).

Each major temple was dedicated to a particular god or group of gods and was considered the god's earthly dwelling place. The temple contained a sanctuary with a statue of the god, which was not merely a representation but a physical focus through which the god's presence manifested on earth. Only priests could enter the sanctuary. Common people couldn't enter the temple's interior but could worship at the temple's outer courts and gates.

Priests served the gods through daily rituals. They woke the god's statue each morning, washed and dressed it, offered it food and drink, and performed ceremonies to maintain ma'at. The priests didn't preach or provide moral instruction. They performed rituals to ensure the proper relationship between gods and humans through the correct performance of ceremonies.

The pharaoh was technically the chief priest of all gods. In temple reliefs and texts, the pharaoh is always shown performing rituals, but usually it was priests acting on his behalf. The pharaoh's divine nature made him the ideal intermediary between the human and divine realms.

Religious festivals brought the gods directly to the people. During festivals, the god's statue would be carried out of the temple on a sacred boat or portable shrine, marched through the streets, and sometimes traveled by river to visit other temples. These processions allowed ordinary Egyptians to see (or at least be near) the god and participate in a religious celebration. Festivals included music, dancing, feasting, and sometimes consultations where people could ask the god questions. The god's response was interpreted through the movements of the sacred barque (boat) carried by the priests.

The Egyptian religion didn't have a rigid doctrine that everyone had to believe. Different cities and regions had different myths about creation and different understandings of the gods. In one region, the world emerged from the primordial waters; in another, it was created by a god's thought and word; in another, it came from a cosmic egg. Egyptians didn't see these contradictions as problems. These different myths could all be true in different ways.

What mattered more was performing the proper rituals, maintaining ma'at, showing respect to the gods, and ensuring the cosmic order continued. At its core, the Egyptian religion was about maintaining the world as it should be, keeping chaos at bay, and ensuring the sun rose, the Nile flooded, and life continued.

Death and the Journey Beyond

Death wasn't the end for ancient Egyptians; it was just a transition to another form of existence. Egyptians devoted enormous resources and attention to preparing for death and guaranteeing a successful afterlife. This preoccupation with death and the afterlife produced some of Egypt's most famous monuments and artifacts, from pyramids to mummies to the *Book of the Dead.*

The Egyptian concept of the person was complex. A person consisted of multiple components, including the physical body, the *ka* (life force or spiritual double), the *ba* (personality or soul that could travel between the living world and the afterlife), the *akh* (transfigured spirit of the successful deceased), the name, and the shadow. All these components needed to be preserved and cared for to ensure a successful existence in the afterlife.

When someone died, their greatest fear was complete oblivion—what Egyptians called the "second death." To avoid this, the dead needed their body preserved, their name remembered, offerings made to sustain them, and successful passage through the dangers of the underworld to reach the realm of Osiris.

Mummification was the process of preserving the body. Egyptians believed the body needed to remain intact for the afterlife. The *ba* needed the body as an anchor to return to, and the deceased would need their body in the afterlife. Initially, natural desiccation in Egypt's hot, dry sand preserved bodies buried in simple graves. However, as elites began building elaborate tombs, artificial preservation became necessary.

The mummification process, as described by the Greek historian Herodotus and confirmed by modern scientific studies, took approximately seventy days and involved several steps.

First, the body was taken to a special workshop, usually located near the tomb or in the desert. Embalmers washed the body with water and wine.

Next, they removed the internal organs, which would decay quickly. Using a hook, they extracted the brain through the nose. The brain wasn't considered important, so it was discarded. They made an incision in the left side of the abdomen and removed the stomach, intestines, liver, and lungs. In earlier periods, these organs were treated, wrapped, and placed in canopic jars, though by the Twenty-first Dynasty and later, practices changed, with organs sometimes placed back in the body and canopic jars serving more of a ceremonial function. The heart was always left in the body; it was considered the seat of intelligence and emotion, and it would be needed for judgment in the afterlife.

The body was then covered and packed with natron, a naturally occurring salt that drew out all moisture. The body remained buried in natron for about forty days, becoming completely desiccated.

After the natron treatment, embalmers washed the body again and rubbed it with oils and resins to keep the skin supple. They sometimes stuffed the body cavity with linen, sawdust, or even sand to maintain the body's shape. They would also pack linen under the skin of the face and limbs to create a more lifelike appearance.

The entire body was then wrapped in hundreds of yards of linen bandages. Between the layers of bandages, embalmers placed protective amulets—small charms of various gods and symbols believed to protect the deceased. A heart scarab was often placed over the heart, inscribed with a spell from the *Book of the Dead* asking the heart not to testify against its owner during judgment.

Finally, the wrapped mummy was placed in one or more coffins. Elite individuals might have multiple nested coffins, with the innermost being human-shaped and decorated with religious texts and images. The mummy was then placed in a tomb along with grave goods—objects the deceased would need in the afterlife.

What objects went into the tomb? It depended on the person's wealth and status, but tombs typically contained the following:

- Food and drink for the deceased's sustenance. These were real provisions, but they were also represented in paintings on tomb walls. The deceased could magically consume the essence of these offerings.

- Clothing, furniture, jewelry, and personal possessions that the deceased had used in life and would need in the afterlife.

- Shabtis (also called ushabtis)—small figurines that would magically come to life and perform labor on behalf of the deceased in the afterlife. The deceased might need to work in the fields of the afterlife, so they brought magical servants to do it for them. Elite tombs might contain hundreds of shabtis.

- Protective amulets and magical texts to help the deceased navigate the dangers of the underworld.

- The *Book of the Dead*—a collection of spells, hymns, and instructions to help the deceased in the afterlife. Despite the name, it wasn't a single book but a compilation of texts that could be selected and customized for each person. These spells were written on papyrus and placed in the tomb or painted on tomb walls or coffins.

However, having a preserved body and grave goods wasn't enough. The deceased still had to successfully navigate the underworld—the Duat—and pass judgment before Osiris.

The journey through the Duat was dangerous. The deceased had to pass through gates guarded by fearsome demons, travel across lakes of fire, avoid monsters and hostile spirits, and speak the correct passwords and spells. The *Book of the Dead* provided guidance for this journey, including illustrations and vignettes, spells for protection, and the secret names of the guardians who had to be appeased.

The culmination of the journey was the judgment before Osiris. This scene is depicted in countless tomb paintings and *Book of the Dead* illustrations. The deceased's heart—the seat of their conscience and moral character—was weighed on a scale against the feather of Ma'at, the symbol of truth and justice. Anubis operated the scales, while Thoth recorded the result.

If the heart was heavy with sin and wrongdoing, it would outweigh the feather. The deceased would then be devoured by Ammit, a monster combining features of a crocodile, lion, and hippopotamus, who waited beside the scales. These people would experience no afterlife.

But if the heart balanced with the feather or was lighter—proving the deceased had lived justly and according to ma'at—they would be declared "justified" or "true of voice." Osiris would welcome them into the afterlife, a paradise called the Field of Reeds, which was imagined as an idealized version of Egypt with abundant harvests, no suffering, and eternal existence in the presence of the gods.

A depiction of the Field of Reeds.[48]

The Field of Reeds was depicted in tomb paintings as a pleasant place resembling the best aspects of earthly Egypt. The deceased would farm, but crops would grow effortlessly. The people would feast but never be hungry. They could enjoy all earthly pleasures without earthly limitations. The blessed dead could also accompany Ra on his solar boat, traveling across the sky each day and through the underworld each night.

Not everyone could afford elaborate mummification and tomb goods. Ordinary Egyptians did their best with simpler burials, but they still sought to preserve the body and provide for the afterlife. Even the poorest Egyptians would try to provide at least a minimal burial, believing that an improper burial condemned the deceased to wander as a restless, suffering ghost.

The living had ongoing obligations to the dead. Family members were supposed to make regular offerings at the tomb—food, drink, and incense—to sustain the deceased's *ka*. The tomb chapel was designed as a place where the living could interact with the dead. Many tombs include a "false door"—a carved representation of a door through which the *ka* could pass between the tomb and the offering chapel, allowing the deceased to receive offerings.

Egyptians could also communicate with the dead through letters. People would write letters on pottery or papyrus, place them in tombs, and ask the deceased for help with problems, like legal issues, illness, or family conflicts. The dead were believed to have power to influence events in the living world, either for good or ill.

This elaborate concern with death and the afterlife wasn't morbid. By preparing for the afterlife, Egyptians were ensuring that life continued forever. Death was just a transition, not an end.

Tombs for Eternity

The evolution of Egyptian tombs reflects changing ideas about the afterlife, available resources, and the problem of tomb robbery. From simple pit graves to massive pyramids to hidden rock-cut chambers, Egyptian tombs were designed to preserve the body, protect it from robbers, and provide for the deceased's eternal needs.

The earliest Egyptian burials were simple graves in the desert sand. The body, wrapped in animal skins or matting, was placed in a shallow pit with a few personal possessions. The hot, dry sand naturally preserved the body through desiccation. These accidental mummies likely inspired later deliberate mummification techniques.

During the Predynastic and Early Dynastic periods, elite burials became more elaborate. Important people were buried in mastabas—rectangular mudbrick structures with flat roofs and sloping sides. The word *mastaba* comes from the Arabic word for "bench" because these tombs resembled the benches outside Egyptian houses.

A mastaba's underground burial chamber contained the body and grave goods, while the aboveground structure contained a chapel where offerings could be made. The burial chamber was sealed after the funeral, but family members could visit the chapel to make offerings and communicate with the deceased. Mastabas could be quite large, with multiple rooms for storing grave goods and elaborate painted or carved decorations.

Example of a mastaba."

The Step Pyramid of Djoser at Saqqara, built around 2670 BCE, revolutionized tomb architecture. The architect Imhotep essentially stacked six mastabas of decreasing size on top of one another, creating a stepped pyramid about two hundred feet high. This was the first large-scale stone building in Egypt and became the prototype for later pyramids.

The true pyramids—with smooth sides meeting at a point—developed shortly after. The great pyramids of Giza, built for the pharaohs Khufu, Khafre, and Menkaure during the Fourth Dynasty (around 2580-2510 BCE), represent the peak of pyramid construction.

But why pyramids? The pyramid shape had a symbolic meaning related to the sun and creation. The pyramid was associated with the *benben* stone, the primordial mound that emerged from the waters of chaos at creation. The pyramid's shape also resembled the rays of the sun descending to earth. Pyramids were essentially elaborate tombs that glorified the pharaoh and ensured his successful journey to the afterlife, where he would join the sun god Ra.

Pyramids were surrounded by complexes, including temples, causeways, and additional structures. The valley temple at the pyramid base conducted funerary rituals. A causeway connected the valley temple to the mortuary temple on the pyramid's east side, where daily offerings were made. There were also smaller pyramids for queens and storage pits for boats.

Pyramids contained burial chambers accessed by narrow passages. These passages were blocked with massive granite blocks after the funeral to prevent tomb robbery. The burial chamber contained the pharaoh's sarcophagus and originally held grave goods, though items might be stored in adjacent rooms or in the temples.

However, pyramids had a flaw: they were obvious targets for tomb robbers. A massive stone structure essentially announced the location of the pharaoh's treasures. Despite elaborate security measures, including false passages, hidden chambers, and massive blocking stones, almost all pyramids were robbed in antiquity, most within a few centuries of their construction.

By the Middle Kingdom, pharaohs experimented with other approaches. Some built smaller, less conspicuous pyramids. Others built elaborate complexes with hidden burial chambers accessible through confusing mazes of passages. But robbers still found the burial chambers, driving New Kingdom pharaohs to try something radically different: complete concealment.

The Valley of the Kings is a remote, narrow valley on the west bank of the Nile across from Thebes (modern Luxor). Here, pharaohs from the Eighteenth through the Twentieth Dynasties (roughly 1550–1070 BCE) were buried in rock-cut tombs carved deep into the valley's limestone cliffs.

A view of the Valley of the Kings."

Instead of advertising the location with a massive pyramid, pharaohs built hidden tombs whose entrances were sealed and camouflaged. The mortuary temples, where offerings were made, were built separately in the valley below. Theoretically, no one would know where the tomb was located except the priests responsible for the burial.

The tombs were elaborate. A corridor descended into the rock, sometimes over two hundred feet down, passing through multiple chambers before reaching the burial chamber. The walls were covered with painted scenes and texts from the *Book of the Dead*, the *Amduat* (a text describing Ra's journey through the night), and other religious texts. The burial chamber contained the pharaoh's stone sarcophagus and nested coffins.

But even concealment failed. The Valley of the Kings was thoroughly plundered in ancient times, probably by the very workmen who built the tombs and lower officials who knew their locations. Court records preserve trials where captured robbers described breaking into tombs, stripping mummies of their gold, and melting down priceless artifacts. By the Third Intermediate Period, priests collected the royal mummies from their plundered tombs and reburied them in hidden locations for protection. Two major groups of royal mummies were discovered in modern times—one in 1881 at Deir el-Bahari, a formal cache containing over fifty royal mummies, and another in 1898 in the tomb of Amenhotep II, which had been reused as a repository for additional royal burials. These discoveries preserved the mummies of some of Egypt's greatest pharaohs, including Ramesses II, Seti I, Thutmose III, and many others. Only one royal tomb in the Valley of the Kings survived largely intact into modern times—Tutankhamun's.

Queens and high officials also had elaborate tombs. The Valley of the Queens, adjacent to the Valley of the Kings, contained tombs for royal wives and children. The tomb of Nefertari, the favorite wife of Ramesses II, features some of the most beautiful tomb paintings in Egypt—vibrant scenes of the queen in the afterlife, meeting gods, playing the board game senet, and journeying through the Duat.

High officials and nobles built tombs appropriate to their status. They were typically smaller than royal tombs but often elaborately decorated. These tombs provide invaluable information about daily life in ancient Egypt. Tomb paintings show farming, hunting, banqueting, and other activities the deceased enjoyed and wanted to continue in the afterlife.

Tomb robbery wasn't just a problem in ancient times. After Egypt fell to foreign powers and the knowledge of hieroglyphics was lost, tombs became treasure troves for antiquity hunters. European collectors in the 18th and 19th centuries acquired thousands of artifacts from plundered tombs. Mummies were ground up for medicine or unwrapped at parties as entertainment. Countless artifacts were destroyed or lost.

Modern archaeology has tried to recover what remains and study tombs scientifically. Archaeological excavations have revealed much about ancient Egyptian funerary practices, religious beliefs, and daily life. Conservation efforts work to preserve tomb paintings and structures damaged by time, humidity, tourists, and ancient vandalism.

Egyptian tombs, whether pyramids at Giza or rock-cut chambers in the Valley of the Kings, demonstrate the Egyptians' conviction that death was not the end. These structures, filled with precious goods and covered with beautiful art and sacred texts, were meant to last forever. They were supposed to be houses for eternity, where the deceased could exist for millions of years. That many have survived for millennia, allowing us to learn about and marvel at ancient Egyptian civilization, would surely please the ancient Egyptians who built them.

Chapter 16:
Daily Life Along the Nile

Society and Social Classes

Egyptian society was hierarchical, with clear distinctions between social classes. Yet compared to many ancient civilizations, Egyptian society offered some degree of social mobility. Even ordinary Egyptians had legal rights and protections, which was unusual for the ancient world.

At the top of the social pyramid stood the pharaoh. He wasn't just a king; he was considered divine. The pharaoh served as the earthly intermediary between humans and the divine realm. The pharaoh owned all of Egypt in theory, though in practice, he delegated authority to administrators. His role was to maintain ma'at through proper rule and religious observance.

The royal family came next—the pharaoh's wives, children, and close relatives. The Great Royal Wife (the pharaoh's principal queen) held considerable status and sometimes wielded real power. Royal children were educated at court and prepared for lives of privilege and responsibility.

Below the royal family were the nobles and high officials. These were the people who actually ran Egypt—viziers who oversaw the government, treasurers who managed finances, generals who commanded armies, and provincial governors who ruled regions on the pharaoh's behalf. These positions were often hereditary, with sons following fathers into office, creating families that maintained power across generations. However, capable commoners could sometimes rise through merit, particularly through military service or scribal training.

Priests formed another important group. Egypt's temples controlled vast lands, wealth, and labor forces. High priests of major temples, particularly the high priest of Amun at Thebes, were among the most powerful people in Egypt. Priests weren't necessarily religious in our modern sense; many were administrators and ritual specialists who served the gods by correctly performing ceremonies. Many priesthood positions were hereditary or appointed, and many were part-time roles, with priests serving in rotating shifts while also pursuing other careers.

Scribes were the educated class who could read and write hieroglyphics, hieratic (the cursive script used for everyday writing), and later demotic (an even more simplified script). Literacy rates in ancient Egypt were probably around 1 to 3 percent of the population, making scribes extremely valuable. They served as administrators, accountants, record-keepers, tax collectors, and bureaucrats. The position of scribe was highly respected and offered a path to advancement.

Soldiers formed a significant class, particularly during the New Kingdom when Egypt maintained a standing army. Egyptian soldiers received land grants and payment in rations. Military service offered opportunities for advancement; successful soldiers could become officers or even high officials. Egypt also employed foreign mercenaries, particularly Nubians and later Greeks, who often settled in Egypt and formed their own communities.

Artisans and craftsmen formed the middle of society. These included sculptors, painters, carpenters, jewelers, potters, metalworkers, weavers, and countless other specialized trades. Skilled craftsmen, particularly those working on royal tombs and monuments, could be quite prosperous and respected. The workers who built the royal tombs in the Valley of the Kings lived in a special village, Deir el-Medina, where they received good wages and enjoyed comfortable lives. Archaeological excavations of this village have provided remarkable detail about the lives of these skilled workers.

The ruins of Deir el-Medina.⁴⁶

At the base of the social pyramid were farmers—the vast majority of Egypt's population. Most farmland was controlled by the pharaoh, temples, or nobles, though some Egyptians, especially in later periods, did hold private land. Farmers who worked state or temple land had hereditary rights to farm it and paid taxes by giving a portion of their harvest. Farming was hard, repetitive work, but farmers generally had enough to eat and lived in stable communities.

Below farmers were laborers—people without land who worked for daily wages on construction projects, in workshops, or wherever temporary labor was needed. And at the very bottom were slaves. Foreign prisoners of war were enslaved and put to work on state projects, in households, or on temple estates, and their treatment could be harsh. Some Egyptians entered servitude because of debt. The status and treatment of enslaved people varied considerably; some had limited rights and could own property, while others lived in conditions closer to chattel slavery. True chattel slavery—people as complete property with no rights—existed but was not the predominant form throughout Egyptian history.

Egyptian society had surprisingly progressive attitudes toward women compared to most ancient civilizations. Egyptian women had extensive legal rights that would have been unusual in Greece or Rome. Women could own property in their own names, inherit wealth, initiate divorce, conduct business, serve as witnesses in court, and make contracts. Documents survive showing women buying and selling property, running businesses, and pursuing legal cases.

Women's primary social role was wife and mother, but this didn't prevent them from having economic independence. Many women worked as weavers, bakers, brewers, musicians, dancers, and in various trades. Upper-class women could own estates and businesses. Women could serve as priestesses, particularly in the cults of female deities. And while extremely rare, women could sometimes become pharaohs.

Children were highly valued in Egyptian society. Having children, especially sons, ensured that someone would care for parents in old age and make offerings to their spirits after death. Daughters were also valued, and Egyptian art frequently shows affection between parents and children. Children of elite families received an education. Boys trained for their future careers as scribes, priests, or officials, while girls learned household management and sometimes received an education in reading and music.

Social mobility existed but was limited. Most people were born into their social class and remained there. Egyptian society valued stability and tradition. Everyone had their place, and maintaining that order was part of maintaining ma'at.

Home, Family, and Food

Most Egyptians lived in houses built of mudbrick—the most practical building material in a land with little timber or stone for construction. Mudbrick was cheap, readily available (made from Nile mud mixed with straw), and well suited to Egypt's climate. It kept homes cool in summer and warm in winter. The downside was that mudbrick deteriorated relatively quickly, which is why relatively few ancient Egyptian houses survived.

Ordinary houses were typically small and simple. A typical farmer's house might have just three or four rooms—a main living area, a storage room, and one or two small bedrooms. The flat roof served as an additional living space, especially in hot weather. Houses were often built close together in villages, with narrow streets winding between them. Archaeological excavations at sites like Deir el-Medina show what workers' villages looked like—rows of similar houses built to a standard plan.

Elite houses were much larger and more elaborate. A wealthy official's house might have dozens of rooms organized around courtyards. These houses included separate areas for men and women, servants' quarters, storage magazines, and workshops. The houses were decorated with painted walls, had multiple stories, and included bathrooms and private shrines. The garden was an important feature. It provided a cool place in Egypt's heat, often with a pool stocked with fish and surrounded by trees and flowers.

Furniture was relatively simple, even in wealthy homes. Egyptians sat on stools, chairs, or cushions on the floor. They slept on beds—wooden frames with woven reed or leather supports, covered with linen sheets and sometimes mosquito netting. Wealthier people had headrests rather than pillows. These curved supports kept the head elevated while protecting elaborate hairstyles. They stored things in wooden chests or large ceramic jars. Oil lamps provided light after dark.

Houses usually had a kitchen area, though it was often outside or in a separate building to keep heat and smoke away from living areas. Cooking was done over open fires or in clay ovens. Most cooking vessels were pottery of various sizes.

The Egyptian diet was based on bread and beer—the two staples that provided most calories for most people. Bread came in many varieties, from coarse loaves for ordinary people to fine white bread for the wealthy. Egyptian bread was made from emmer wheat or barley. It was often quite coarse, containing grit from the grinding stones, which wore down people's teeth.

Beer was the everyday drink for all social classes, including children. Egyptian beer was nutritious and relatively low in alcohol—it was more like liquid bread than modern beer. It was made from barley or emmer wheat, partially baked into loaves, then crumbled into water and allowed to ferment. The result was a thick, sweet, slightly alcoholic beverage that was drunk through straws to filter out the grain particles.

Vegetables were also important. Onions, garlic, leeks, lettuce, cucumbers, and beans were common. Fruits included dates, figs, grapes, melons, and pomegranates.

Meat was a luxury for most people, though elites ate it regularly. Egyptians raised cattle, sheep, goats, and pigs. Poultry—ducks, geese, and domesticated chickens (in later periods)—provided both meat and eggs. Wealthy households might have elaborate farms that raised various animals. Ordinary people ate meat mainly on festival days or special occasions, though they might keep a few chickens or a goat.

Fish from the Nile were an important protein source, especially for ordinary Egyptians. The Nile teemed with fish, and fishing was a common activity. Fish could be eaten fresh, dried, or salted. However, some fish were considered sacred and forbidden to eat in certain regions. Some priesthoods forbade fish consumption due to local religious traditions.

Wild birds, like ducks and geese, could be hunted in the marshes. Wealthy Egyptians enjoyed hunting expeditions in the papyrus marshes, using throwing sticks to bring down birds, though this was as much sport as food gathering.

Food was seasoned with salt, honey, and various herbs and spices. Olive oil (in later periods) and other oils were used for cooking and as condiments. Wine was made from grapes or dates, but it was more expensive than beer and typically drunk by the wealthy.

Egyptians ate two or three meals a day. A simple breakfast might be bread and beer. The main meal, eaten in the afternoon or evening, might include bread, beer, vegetables, and perhaps fish or meat if available. Wealthier people enjoyed more elaborate meals with multiple courses, served on fine pottery or even metal dishes.

Extended families often lived in close proximity, with married sons building houses near their parents. Family ties were strong. Egyptian texts emphasize the importance of respecting parents and repaying them for raising you.

Children worked from an early age, helping with household tasks and learning the skills they would need as adults. But Egyptian children knew how to play. They played with dolls, balls, spinning tops, toy animals, and board games. They also played physical games—wrestling, running, and various ball games.

Life expectancy was short by modern standards—perhaps thirty-five to forty years on average—and childhood mortality was high. But for those who survived childhood, life could be reasonably comfortable, especially in times of prosperity.

Work, Play, and Leisure

The rhythm of Egyptian life followed the agricultural calendar, which in turn followed the Nile's annual cycle. The Egyptian year was divided into three seasons of four months each: Akhet (inundation), Peret (growing), and Shemu (harvest).

During Akhet (roughly July to October), the Nile flooded, covering the fields with water and depositing fresh silt. This was the time when farmers couldn't work their fields, so the state mobilized laborers for construction projects. The great pyramids and temples were built during the inundation season. This wasn't slavery but a form of taxation—able-bodied men served the state with their labor for part of the year and were fed and housed while doing so.

During Peret (roughly November to February), the floodwaters receded, leaving the fields covered with fresh, fertile silt. Farmers plowed the soft ground, often using wooden plows pulled by cattle, and planted seeds. This was the season of hope. If the Nile had flooded properly, crops would grow well, and there would be plenty to eat. If the flooding had been insufficient, there could have been famine.

During Shemu (roughly March to June), the crops matured and were harvested. This was the busiest season for farmers. Grain had to be cut with sickles, threshed to separate grain from chaff, and stored. Tax collectors came to measure the harvest and take the state's share.

Craftsmen worked year-round in workshops. The workshops at Deir el-Medina, where tomb workers lived, show how organized craft work was. Workers received regular rations in exchange for their labor. They worked in teams on specific projects, with foremen supervising and scribes recording everything.

The workweek varied by occupation and period. Evidence from the New Kingdom royal tomb workers suggests a ten-day cycle, with one day off after each ten-day period—a more grueling schedule than our modern five-day workweek. However, religious festivals were frequent and provided additional days off. Between regular days off and festival days, workers probably had roughly sixty to seventy days off per year, though this varied considerably by occupation and period.

Traders traveled up and down the Nile and to foreign lands, exchanging Egyptian grain, linen, and papyrus for luxury goods like incense, ebony, and precious metals. Physicians practiced medicine, using a combination of practical treatments and magic. Teachers educated the children of elites. Servants worked in wealthy households. Fishermen worked the Nile. Builders constructed houses and monuments. Weavers made linen cloth, Egypt's main textile, from flax grown along the Nile. Scribes recorded everything, from tax records to inventory lists. Training to be a scribe took years since they had to learn hundreds of hieroglyphic signs and the cursive hieratic script. Scribal schools used corporal punishment liberally. Texts say teachers threatened to beat lazy students until "their backs listened."

Egyptians still found time for leisure and entertainment. Music and dance were important parts of Egyptian life. Musicians played harps, lutes, lyres, flutes, drums, and other instruments at festivals, banquets, and religious ceremonies. Professional musicians and dancers performed at wealthy households. Music was also important in religious rituals, as priests and priestesses sang hymns to the gods.

Board games were popular. The most famous was senet, a game played on a rectangular board with thirty squares, using stick dice or throwing sticks to determine moves. Senet had religious significance—it was associated with the journey to the afterlife—but it was also played for fun. Other games included mehen (a snake-shaped board game) and a game similar to checkers.

Egyptians enjoyed physical activities and sports. Hunting was popular among the wealthy; pharaohs and nobles hunted dangerous game like lions, wild bulls, and hippopotamuses in the desert and marshes. Fishing and fowling in the marshes were enjoyed by all social classes.

Wrestling was a popular sport, with tournaments and competitions. Swimming was also popular. Running races, stick fighting, and various ball games were played. Children played versions of leapfrog, tug-of-war, and other physical games still played today.

Banquets were important social occasions for the elite. Tomb paintings often depict lavish feasts with guests dressed in fine linen, wearing elaborate wigs and jewelry, and sitting on cushioned chairs while servants bring food and drink. Musicians and dancers entertained. Guests ate, drank wine and beer, conversed, and sometimes got quite drunk. Some banquet scenes show guests vomiting from excess, suggesting Egyptians enjoyed their parties.

Festivals broke the routine of work and provided a community celebration. Major religious festivals could last days or weeks. The Beautiful Feast of the Valley at Thebes involved processions of the gods' statues, offerings at tombs, family gatherings at ancestral graves, and feasting. The Opet Festival at Thebes celebrated the annual flooding of the Nile with processions, music, and celebration. Festivals included food, beer, music, dancing, and opportunities to participate in or witness religious rituals.

Egyptian culture valued joy and celebration, and Egyptian art and texts suggest people found pleasure in family, food, music, festivals, and the beauty of the Nile Valley. The Egyptian concept of the afterlife as an idealized version of earthly life suggests they thought life was good and worth preserving eternally.

Of course, life could be hard. Droughts, poor floods, diseases, accidents, warfare, and oppressive taxation could make life miserable. Not everyone was content with their place in society. Legal documents preserve complaints of corruption, unfair treatment, and other injustices. Life for ordinary Egyptians was often difficult and shaped by forces beyond their control—the Nile's flooding, the demands of the state, and the decisions of distant rulers.

But within these constraints, Egyptians built meaningful lives. They worked, raised families, worshiped their gods, celebrated festivals, enjoyed simple pleasures, and hoped for a good afterlife. They left behind not just monuments and mummies but also traces of everyday existence—letters, shopping lists, work logs, school exercises, love poems, jokes, and complaints. These glimpses of daily life show that ancient Egyptians weren't so different from us. They worried about their jobs, complained about their bosses, loved their families, enjoyed parties, and tried to find meaning and happiness in their brief time on earth.

Chapter 17:
Egyptian Innovations and Legacy

Writing, Science, and Medicine

Ancient Egypt made fundamental contributions to civilization that still influence us today. Egyptian innovations in writing, mathematics, engineering, and medicine laid the groundwork for later developments. While the Egyptians weren't alone in developing these technologies—other ancient civilizations made similar advances—Egyptian achievements were remarkable.

The most visible Egyptian innovation was writing. Egyptian hieroglyphics are among the world's oldest writing systems, developing around 3200 BCE. The word "hieroglyphics" comes from Greek words meaning "sacred carvings," and that's what they were—a writing system used primarily for religious and monumental inscriptions.

Hieroglyphics used hundreds of symbols representing sounds, ideas, or both. Some signs were phonetic, representing sounds like letters or syllables. Others were ideograms, representing whole words or concepts. Still others were determinatives, signs added at the end of words to clarify meaning.

Hieroglyphics were too elaborate for everyday use. For business, letters, and administrative records, Egyptians developed hieratic script—a cursive, simplified form of hieroglyphics that could be written quickly with a reed pen and ink on papyrus. Hieratic developed early in Egyptian history and was used throughout the pharaonic period for practical documents.

Later, around 650 BCE, an even more simplified script called demotic emerged. Demotic was faster to write and became the common script for everyday documents in the Late Period. Egypt primarily used hieroglyphics for religious and monumental texts; hieratic for religious texts (especially funerary papyri), literary manuscripts, and administrative documents for most of Egyptian history; and demotic for daily business and legal documents in later periods. Hieratic continued to be used for religious purposes even after demotic emerged for administrative use.

Egyptian writing was forgotten after Egypt became Christian and adopted Greek and Coptic scripts. The ability to read hieroglyphics was lost by the 4th or 5th century CE. For over 1,400 years, Egyptian hieroglyphics remained indecipherable. They were beautiful but mysterious symbols that no one could read.

The breakthrough came in 1799 when French soldiers in Egypt discovered the Rosetta Stone, a granite slab inscribed with the same text in three scripts: hieroglyphics, demotic, and ancient Greek. Since scholars could read Greek, they had a key to deciphering the other scripts. French scholar Jean-François Champollion finally cracked the code in 1822, using the Rosetta Stone and other bilingual texts to work out how hieroglyphics represented sounds and meanings. This breakthrough opened up Egyptian civilization to modern understanding, allowing scholars to learn about Egyptian history, religion, and culture directly from Egyptian sources.

Egyptian mathematics was practical rather than theoretical. Egyptians needed math for surveying land, calculating taxes, planning construction, measuring grain, and managing resources. They developed a decimal system based on powers of ten, with distinct symbols for one, ten, one hundred, one thousand, and so on.

Egyptian mathematics used addition and multiplication as primary operations. They performed multiplication through repeated doubling—a method that's actually quite efficient. For example, to multiply 13 by 7, they would double 13 repeatedly (13, 26, 52, 104) and then select the appropriate values—in this case 52 + 26 + 13—to reach the correct total of 91. Division worked similarly, as repeated doubling in reverse.

For fractions, Egyptians had an unusual system. They used only unit fractions (fractions with 1 as the numerator, like 1/2, 1/3, 1/4). To express other fractions, they combined unit fractions. So, 3/4 would be written as 1/2 + 1/4. This seems awkward to us, but Egyptian scribes became very skilled at working with them.

Egyptian geometry was also advanced for the time. Surveyors needed to reestablish field boundaries after the annual Nile flood washed away markers. Architects needed to calculate volumes and angles for construction. The Egyptians developed formulas for calculating areas of rectangles, triangles, and circles and volumes of cylinders and pyramids. Their formula for the area of a circle was remarkably accurate. They approximated pi as approximately 3.16, which is close to the true value of 3.14159.

The construction of the pyramids demonstrates sophisticated engineering and mathematical knowledge. The Great Pyramid of Khufu is aligned to true north with remarkable precision; it is just 3/60 of a degree off. The base is nearly perfectly square, with sides differing by less than 2 inches out of over 750 feet. The angles of the faces are precisely calculated to meet at the apex. Achieving this level of accuracy with ancient tools required detailed mathematical planning and surveying.

Egyptian astronomy focused on creating a workable calendar. Egyptians developed a solar calendar of 365 days, which was divided into 12 months of 30 days each, plus 5 extra days. This calendar was remarkably accurate and served as the basis for later calendars, including our modern calendar. Egyptians also observed the stars. They recognized constellations and used stellar observations for timekeeping and to predict the Nile's flooding. The heliacal rising of Sirius (the star's first appearance on the eastern horizon just before dawn) originally coincided with the beginning of the Nile's annual flood, providing a natural marker for the new year. However, because the 365-day calendar lacked a leap year, this coincidence drifted by one day every four years, a discrepancy the Egyptians were aware of.

Egyptian medicine was a mixture of practical treatments and magical spells. Medical papyri survive that describe treatments for various ailments, showing that Egyptian physicians had considerable practical knowledge. Egyptian doctors could set broken bones and immobilize them with splints. They could stitch wounds and perform minor surgery. They extracted teeth and treated wounds with honey (which has natural antibacterial properties, though Egyptians didn't know this; they just used it because it worked). They prescribed various herbal remedies, some of which had genuine medicinal value.

The Edwin Smith Papyrus, dating to around 1600 BCE but copied from older material, is a surgical textbook describing forty-eight cases of injuries and wounds, primarily to the head and torso. For each case, it provides a systematic examination procedure, diagnosis, prognosis, and treatment. The text is remarkably rational, with relatively few magical elements (though some spells are included, particularly for untreatable cases). It distinguishes between injuries that can be treated, injuries that might be treated, and injuries that are untreatable.

The Ebers Papyrus, also from around 1600 BCE, is more comprehensive, covering a wider range of ailments, including internal diseases, skin conditions, eye problems, and gynecological issues. It includes over eight hundred remedies using various plants, minerals, and animal products. Some of these remedies had genuine medicinal properties, such as willow bark (which contains a compound related to aspirin), honey, and various herbs with known therapeutic effects. Others were probably ineffective or even harmful.

Many treatments included spells and incantations along with physical remedies. Egyptians believed that some illnesses were caused by demons or angry spirits, so magical protection was necessary. They wore amulets to protect against disease. They recited spells while applying medicine. This combination of practical treatment and magic seems strange to us, but for Egyptians, the physical and spiritual were interconnected.

Egyptian medical knowledge spread throughout the ancient Mediterranean world primarily through cultural contact rather than direct translation of texts. Greek physicians acknowledged learning from Egyptian medical traditions. The reputation of Egyptian medicine was so high that foreign rulers sometimes requested Egyptian doctors.

The Long Shadow of the Pharaohs

Ancient Egypt has fascinated people for thousands of years, and that fascination has profoundly influenced Western culture and imagination. From ancient Greece and Rome through the Renaissance to modern times, Egypt has served as a source of mystery, wisdom, and inspiration.

The ancient Greeks were fascinated by Egypt. Greek scholars, philosophers, and historians traveled to Egypt and wrote about the Egyptian civilization. Herodotus devoted a substantial portion of his *Histories* to Egypt, describing its geography, customs, religion, and monuments. He got some things wrong, but he preserved valuable information. Greek sources claimed that Plato and other philosophers studied with Egyptian priests, though modern scholars view these claims as possibly legendary. Regardless of whether specific individuals actually studied in Egypt, the Greeks clearly viewed Egypt as an ancient land of wisdom and learning.

The Greeks also influenced how we understand Egypt. They gave us the word "pyramid" (from their word for wheat cake, which had a similar shape). They gave us "hieroglyphics" (sacred carvings). They gave us many of the names we use for Egyptian gods; for instance, we call the god Djehuty "Thoth" because that's what the Greeks called him. The Greeks also engaged in syncretism, equating Egyptian gods with their own deities (such as identifying Amun with Zeus), which sometimes distorted the original Egyptian concept. Greek accounts of Egypt, while sometimes inaccurate, preserved knowledge of the Egyptian civilization during the periods when hieroglyphics couldn't be read.

The Romans, after conquering Egypt in 30 BCE, were also fascinated. Wealthy Romans collected Egyptian antiquities. Egyptian art influenced Roman decorative styles. The Romans transported Egyptian obelisks to Rome; several still stand in Rome today, more than remain in Egypt. Egyptian cults, particularly the worship of Isis, spread throughout the Roman Empire. Isis temples were built from Britain to Mesopotamia.

During the Middle Ages, knowledge of ancient Egypt declined in Europe. Egypt was part of the Islamic world, and direct European contact was limited. But Egypt remained a source of mystery and legend. Biblical accounts of Egypt—the Exodus story, Joseph in Egypt, the Flight into Egypt—kept Egypt in the European consciousness. Egypt was imagined as a land of wonders, magic, and ancient secrets.

The Renaissance brought renewed interest in ancient Egypt as Europeans rediscovered classical learning. Scholars studied Greek and Roman accounts of Egypt, and Egyptian artifacts began appearing in European collections. But without the ability to read hieroglyphics, Europeans still couldn't truly understand Egyptian civilization.

Napoleon's invasion of Egypt in 1798 marked a turning point. Napoleon brought scholars and scientists along with his army. They studied, measured, drew, and described Egyptian monuments, producing the massive *Description de l'Égypte* that introduced Egypt to European audiences in unprecedented detail. This expedition also yielded the Rosetta Stone, which would prove crucial to finally deciphering hieroglyphics. After Champollion's breakthrough in 1822, Egyptology emerged as a serious scholarly discipline. European scholars could finally read Egyptian texts, study Egyptian history from Egyptian sources, and begin to understand Egyptian civilization on its own terms rather than through Greek and Roman filters.

The 19th century saw "Egyptomania," a popular fascination with all things Egyptian. Egyptian motifs appeared in architecture, art, fashion, and design. Museums competed to acquire Egyptian artifacts. European and American tourists flocked to Egypt. Archaeological expeditions—some scholarly, others little better than treasure hunting—excavated sites throughout Egypt. Thousands of artifacts were shipped to European and American museums.

This period was problematic in many ways. Archaeological methods were often crude, destroying information. Mummies were unwrapped as public entertainment. Artifacts were scattered across the world, removed from their cultural context. Local Egyptian interests were often ignored. However, this period also established Egyptology as a discipline and brought the ancient Egyptian civilization to worldwide attention.

The 20th century brought more scientific archaeology. Egyptologists developed better methods, asked better questions, and built more complete pictures of the Egyptian civilization. They discovered royal mummy caches, the workers' village at Deir el-Medina, the city of Amarna, and numerous tombs and temples.

Egypt in popular culture has also been influential. Egyptian themes appear constantly in Western art, literature, film, and design. The Art Deco movement of the 1920s incorporated Egyptian motifs. There are Egyptian-themed buildings in cities worldwide. Egyptian symbols appear in jewelry, fashion, and graphic design.

Movies have shaped how people imagine ancient Egypt. Films, from classic Hollywood epics like *The Ten Commandments* to modern blockbusters like *The Mummy*, have depicted Egypt, though usually with more attention to drama than accuracy. These films have created powerful popular images of Egypt that influence how millions of people envision the ancient world.

Egyptian symbolism even appears in unexpected places. The pyramid on the US dollar bill references Egyptian symbolism adopted by Enlightenment thinkers. Obelisks appear in cities worldwide; some are genuine Egyptian obelisks transported abroad, while others are modern copies.

This cultural influence isn't always positive. Popular culture often reduces Egypt to stereotypes—mummies, curses, pyramids in deserts. Many popular depictions of Egypt are historically inaccurate. The fascination with Egypt can become orientalism—imagining Egypt as exotic, mysterious, and other, rather than as a human civilization with complexity.

Modern Egyptology tries to understand ancient Egypt on its own terms, as a real place inhabited by real people, not as a land of mystery and magic. However, the romantic image of Egypt persists, and for many people, Egypt remains a source of fascination, wonder, and imagination.

What We're Still Learning

Despite over two centuries of Egyptology, we're still learning about ancient Egypt. New discoveries continue to surprise scholars. New technologies reveal information invisible to earlier archaeologists. New questions generate new insights.

In 2017, archaeologists discovered a massive statue of Ramesses II submerged in a Cairo slum. The same year, scientists used cosmic-ray muon detectors (essentially imaging empty space inside pyramids using particles from space) to discover a previously unknown large void in the Great Pyramid of Khufu. What this void represents remains unknown, but this technology shows how new methods can reveal new information about even the most studied monuments. In 2019, dozens of sealed coffins were found at Saqqara; they had been untouched for millennia. In 2020, more than one hundred sealed sarcophagi were discovered at Saqqara, containing well-preserved mummies.

Modern technology has revolutionized Egyptology in recent decades. Satellite imagery reveals hidden structures. Ground-penetrating radar maps underground features without excavation. DNA analysis of mummies has revealed family relationships, diseases, and genetic information. Chemical analysis of mummies can determine ancient diets, trace exposure to pollution, and identify causes of death. 3D scanning creates perfect digital records of artifacts and structures.

Climate studies using ice cores, sediment analysis, and other techniques have revealed information about ancient climate, Nile flooding patterns, and environmental changes. These studies help explain historical events. Periods of instability often correlate with poor Nile floods caused by climate change. Understanding ancient climate helps explain the rise and fall of Egyptian power.

New archaeological approaches focus on questions earlier scholars ignored. Recent work examines the daily life of ordinary Egyptians, not just kings and nobles. Studies investigate ancient Egyptian cities, which were less studied than tombs and temples because urban sites are often covered by modern settlements. Research now explores the Egyptian economy, trade networks, and administrative systems. Gender studies examine women's roles in Egyptian society. All these approaches broaden our understanding of ancient Egypt.

We're also reexamining old assumptions. Earlier scholars often simply accepted Greek and Roman accounts of Egypt. Modern Egyptologists read Egyptian sources directly and recognize that Greek and Roman writers sometimes misunderstood or distorted Egyptian culture. Earlier scholars sometimes imposed their own cultural assumptions. Modern scholars try to understand Egypt on its own terms, recognizing their own biases and limitations.

Fundamental questions remain unanswered or debated. How exactly were the pyramids built? We have a general understanding, but specific details of construction methods remain uncertain. The Great Sphinx remains mysterious. When was it carved? Most scholars date it to the reign of Khafre (around 2500 BCE), but some suggest it's older. Who does it represent? Probably Khafre, but this isn't certain. Why was its nose destroyed? We don't know, though various legends exist.

Many aspects of Egyptian religion remain unclear. Egyptian religious texts are often cryptic and symbolic, so they are difficult to interpret definitively. The relationship between different gods, the nature of Egyptian beliefs in the afterlife, and the details of religious rituals are still debated among scholars.

Egyptian history itself has gaps and uncertainties. Chronology is debated. Different scholars propose different dates for various events, sometimes differing by decades or even centuries. Many pharaohs are known only from fragmentary evidence. Entire periods, like the Second Intermediate Period, remain poorly understood. The causes of major historical events, like the Bronze Age Collapse, the fall of the New Kingdom, and the success of Alexander's conquest, remain subjects of scholarly debate.

Conservation is an ongoing challenge. Egyptian monuments and artifacts are threatened by time, environmental damage, tourism, and urban development. The high water table in the Nile Delta poses a threat to archaeological sites. Air pollution in Cairo damages stone monuments. Tourism, while economically important, brings crowds that stress ancient structures. Rising groundwater threatens the Sphinx and nearby monuments. Climate change may affect preservation. Egyptologists work with conservators, engineers, and Egyptian authorities to preserve monuments for future generations.

Today, Egyptian scholars play leading roles; for decades, Egyptology was dominated by Europeans and Americans. International teams from around the world work in Egypt. The field is slowly becoming more diverse in terms of gender and ethnicity, though it still has work to do.

Ancient Egypt continues to surprise, inspire, and challenge us. Despite centuries of study, Egypt hasn't given up all its secrets. Every excavation season brings new finds. Every new technology reveals new information. Every generation of scholars asks new questions and develops new interpretations.

Conclusion:
Three Thousand Years in Perspective

When we step back and look at ancient Egypt's entire sweep of history—from the first unification around 3100 BCE to Cleopatra's death in 30 BCE—we're looking at roughly three thousand years of continuous civilization. To put that in perspective, the entire span from the fall of Rome to today is less than two thousand years. Ancient Egypt lasted longer than most civilizations have even existed.

What made Egypt last so long? Geography provided natural advantages. An effective organization allowed Egyptians to build monuments, maintain armies, and manage resources. Religion provided ideological unity through the concept of ma'at. Their culture valued tradition and continuity. Yet Egypt also adapted when necessary, adopting new technologies and absorbing useful foreign influences while maintaining its core identity.

Of course, Egypt changed considerably over three millennia. The Egypt of the Old Kingdom pyramid builders was quite different from the New Kingdom or the Ptolemaic period. Egypt was never frozen in time; it was a living, changing civilization that showed remarkable resilience, bouncing back from chaos to reunify and rebuild.

Why does Egypt still fascinate us? The monuments that still stand—the pyramids, temples, and tombs—remain impressive after thousands of years. The art is beautiful and instantly recognizable. But Egypt fascinates us for deeper reasons too. It was one of humanity's first great civilizations, demonstrating what organized societies could achieve. And the more we learn, the more familiar the Egyptians seem.

Egypt's three-thousand-year run eventually ended. No civilization lasts forever. But what Egypt achieved—the monuments they built, the knowledge they developed, and the culture they maintained—continues to inspire us. Ancient Egypt is gone, but it hasn't been forgotten, and its story continues to unfold as new discoveries are made and new questions are asked.

Here's another book by Matt Clayton that you might like

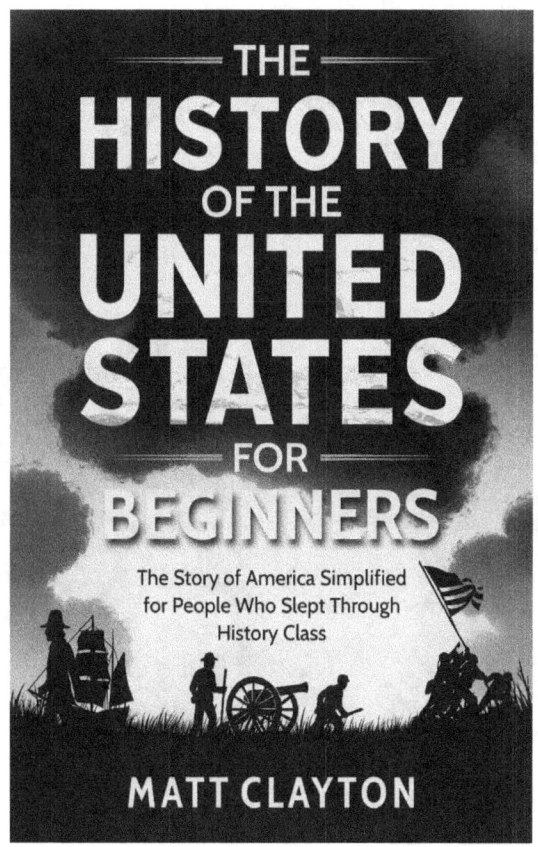

Free Bonus from Captivating History (Available for a Limited time)

Hi History Lovers!

Now you have a chance to join our exclusive history list so you can get your first history ebook for free as well as discounts and a potential to get more history books for free!

Simply visit the link below to join.

Or, Scan the QR code!

captivatinghistory.com/ebook

Also, make sure to follow us on Facebook, X, and YouTube by searching for Captivating History.

References

Assmann, Jan. *Death and Salvation in Ancient Egypt. Translated by David Lorton.* Ithaca: Cornell University Press, 2005.

Bard, Kathryn A. *An Introduction to the Archaeology of Ancient Egypt. 2nd ed.* Oxford: Wiley-Blackwell, 2015.

Cline, Eric H., and David O'Connor, eds. *Thutmose III: A New Biography.* Ann Arbor: University of Michigan Press, 2006.

Grajetzki, Wolfram. *The Middle Kingdom of Ancient Egypt: History, Archaeology and Society.* London: Duckworth, 2006.

Hornung, Erik. *Akhenaten and the Religion of Light. Translated by David Lorton.* Ithaca: Cornell University Press, 1999.

Ikram, Salima. *Death and Burial in Ancient Egypt.* London: Longman, 2003.

Kitchen, Kenneth A. *Pharaoh Triumphant: The Life and Times of Ramesses II, King of Egypt.* Warminster: Aris & Phillips, 1982.

Kemp, Barry J. *Ancient Egypt: Anatomy of a Civilization. 3rd ed.* London: Routledge, 2018.

Lehner, Mark. *The Complete Pyramids.* London: Thames & Hudson, 1997.

Midant-Reynes, Béatrix. *The Prehistory of Egypt: From the First Egyptians to the First Pharaohs. Translated by Ian Shaw.* Oxford: Blackwell Publishers, 2000.

Moran, William L., ed. *The Amarna Letters.* Baltimore: Johns Hopkins University Press, 1992.

Morkot, Robert G. *The Black Pharaohs: Egypt's Nubian Rulers.* London: Rubicon Press, 2000.

Morris, Ellen. *The Architecture of Imperialism: Military Bases and the Evolution of Foreign Policy in Egypt's New Kingdom.* Leiden: Brill, 2005.

O'Connor, David, and Eric H. Cline, eds. *Amenhotep III: Perspectives on His Reign.* Ann Arbor: University of Michigan Press, 1998.

Parkinson, R. B. *The Tale of Sinuhe and Other Ancient Egyptian Poems, 1940–1640 BC.* Oxford: Oxford University Press, 1997.

Quirke, Stephen. *The Administration of Egypt in the Late Middle Kingdom.* New Malden: SIA Publishing, 1990.

Shaw, Ian, ed. *The Oxford History of Ancient Egypt.* Oxford: Oxford University Press, 2000.

Taylor, John H. *Death and the Afterlife in Ancient Egypt.* London: British Museum Press, 2001.

Wilkinson, Richard H. *The Complete Gods and Goddesses of Ancient Egypt.* London: Thames & Hudson, 2003.

Wilkinson, Toby A. H. *Early Dynastic Egypt.* London: Routledge, 1999.

Image Sources

1   Jeff Dahl, CC BY-SA 4.0 <https://creativecommons.org/licenses/by-sa/4.0>, via Wikimedia Commons, https://commons.wikimedia.org /wiki/File:Ancient_Egypt_map-en.svg

2   H.Seldon, CC BY-SA 3.0 <http://creativecommons.org/licenses/by-sa/3.0/>, via Wikimedia Commons, https://commons.wikimedia.org/wiki/File:NaqadaI.svg

3   Metropolitan Museum of Art, CC0, via Wikimedia Commons, https://commons.wikimedia.org/wiki/File:Jar,_Late_Naqada_II,_3500-3300_BCE,_Egypt.jpg

4   Charles J. Sharp, CC BY-SA 3.0 <https://creativecommons.org/licenses/by-sa/3.0>, via Wikimedia Commons, https://commons.wikimedia.org/wiki/File:Saqqara_pyramid_ver_2.jpg

5   Ivrienen at English Wikipedia, CC BY 3.0 <https://creativecommons.org/licenses/by/3.0>, via Wikimedia Commons, https://commons.wikimedia.org/wiki/File:Snefru%27s_Bent_Pyramid_in_Dahshur.jpg

6   Olaf Tausch, CC BY 3.0 <https://creativecommons.org/licenses/by/3.0>, via Wikimedia Commons, https://commons.wikimedia.org/wiki/File:Rote_Pyramide_(Dahschur)_04.jpg

7   KennyOMG, CC BY-SA 4.0 <https://creativecommons.org/licenses/by-sa/4.0>, via Wikimedia Commons, https://commons.wikimedia.org/wiki/File:Pyramids_of_the_Giza_Necropolis.jpg

8   British Museum, CC BY-SA 3.0 <http://creativecommons.org/licenses/by-sa/3.0/>, via Wikimedia Commons, https://commons.wikimedia.org/wiki/File:ThreeStatuesOfSesotrisIII-RightProfiles-BritishMuseum-August19-08.jpg

9   https://www.metmuseum.org/art/collection/search/545728

10 Tim Evanson from Cleveland Heights, Ohio, USA, CC BY-SA 2.0 <https://creativecommons.org/licenses/by-sa/2.0>, via Wikimedia Commons, https://commons.wikimedia.org/wiki/File:Ring_scarab_-_Pharaoh_exhibit_-_Cleveland_Museum_of_Art_(cropped).jpg

11 https://commons.wikimedia.org/wiki/File:Sequenre_tao.JPG

12 Metropolitan Museum of Art, CC0, via Wikimedia Commons, https://commons.wikimedia.org/wiki/File:Seated_Statue_of_Hatshepsut_MET_Hatshepsut2012.jpg

13 Unknown author, CC BY-SA 2.5 <https://creativecommons.org/licenses/by-sa/2.5>, via Wikimedia Commons, https://commons.wikimedia.org/wiki/File:Parehu,_the_Prince_of_Punt,_his_wife_and_his_two_sons,_and_a_daughter._(1902)_-_TIMEA.jpg

14 Diego Delso, CC BY-SA 4.0 <https://creativecommons.org/licenses/by-sa/4.0>, via Wikimedia Commons, https://commons.wikimedia.org/wiki/File:Templo_funerario_de_Hatshepsut,_Luxor,_Egipto,_2022-04-03,_DD_13.jpg

15 https://commons.wikimedia.org/wiki/File:Thutmosis_III-2.jpg

16 Olaf Tausch, CC BY 3.0 <https://creativecommons.org/licenses/by/3.0>, via Wikimedia Commons, https://commons.wikimedia.org/wiki/File:Kom_el-Hettan_24.jpg

17 https://commons.wikimedia.org/wiki/File:Egyptian_-_Commemorative_Scarab_of_Amenhotep_III_-_Walters_42206_-_Bottom.jpg

18 This file is licensed under the Creative Commons Attribution-Share Alike 2.5 Generic license, https://creativecommons.org/licenses/by-sa/2.5/deed.en. https://commons.wikimedia.org/wiki/File:GD-EG-Caire-Mus%C3%A9e061.JPG

19 Osama Shukir Muhammed Amin FRCP(Glasg), CC BY-SA 4.0 <https://creativecommons.org/licenses/by-sa/4.0>, via Wikimedia Commons, https://commons.wikimedia.org/wiki/File:Alabaster_sunken_relief_depicting_Akhenaten,_Nefertiti,_and_daughter_Meritaten._Early_Aten_cartouches_on_king%27s_arm_and_chest._From_Amarna,_Egypt._18th_Dynasty._The_Petrie_Museum_of_Egyptian_Archaeology,_London.jpg

20 Neoclassicism Enthusiast, CC BY-SA 4.0 <https://creativecommons.org/licenses/by-sa/4.0>, via Wikimedia Commons, https://commons.wikimedia.org/wiki/File:Relief_depicting_Akhenaton_and_Nefertiti_with_three_of_their_daughters_under_the_rays_of_Aton_01_(cropped).jpg

21 https://commons.wikimedia.org/wiki/File:CairoEgMuseumTaaMaskMostly Photographed.jpg

22 https://commons.wikimedia.org/wiki/File:Anuk.PNG

23 Museo Egizio In Turin (IT), CC0, via Wikimedia Commons, https://commons.wikimedia.org/wiki/File:Statue_of_king_Horemheb_with_the_god_Amun.png

24 Philip Pikart, CC BY-SA 3.0 <https://creativecommons.org/licenses/by-sa/3.0>, via Wikimedia Commons, https://commons.wikimedia.org/wiki/File: Nofretete_Neues_Museum.jpg

25 Forever Egypt, CC BY-SA 4.0 <https://creativecommons.org/licenses/by-sa/4.0>, via Wikimedia Commons, https://commons.wikimedia.org/wiki/File: Temple_of_Sethi_I_03,_egypt_forever.jpg

26 Carole Raddato from Frankfurt, Germany, CC BY-SA 2.0 <https://creativecommons.org/licenses/by-sa/2.0>, via Wikimedia Commons, https://commons.wikimedia.org/wiki/File:KV17,_the_tomb_of_Pharaoh_Seti_I_of_t he_Nineteenth_Dynasty,_Valley_of_the_Kings,_Egypt_(49846343021).jpg

27 This file is licensed under the Creative Commons Attribution-Share Alike 3.0 Unported license, https://creativecommons.org/licenses/by-sa/3.0/deed.en. https://commons.wikimedia.org/wiki/File:Egypt_Abou_Simbel6.jpg

28 Roland Unger, CC BY-SA 3.0 <https://creativecommons.org/licenses/by-sa/3.0>, via Wikimedia Commons, https://commons.wikimedia.org/wiki/File: RamesseumPM10.jpg

29 youssef_alam, CC BY 3.0 <https://creativecommons.org/licenses/by/3.0>, via Wikimedia Commons, https://commons.wikimedia.org/wiki/File: Ramsis,_Aswan_Governorate,_Egypt_-_panoramio.jpg

30 https://commons.wikimedia.org/wiki/File:Abusimbel.jpg

31 Marc Ryckaert, CC BY-SA 4.0 <https://creativecommons.org/licenses/by-sa/4.0>, via Wikimedia Commons, https://commons.wikimedia.org/wiki/File: Karnak_Hypostyle_Hall_R05.jpg

32 Onceinawhile, CC BY-SA 4.0 <https://creativecommons.org/licenses/by-sa/4.0>, via Wikimedia Commons, https://commons.wikimedia.org/wiki/File: Tomb_of_Nefertari_2022_84.jpg

33 https://commons.wikimedia.org/wiki/File:Medinet_Habu_Ramses_III._ Tempel_Nordostwand_Abzeichnung_01.jpg

34 Original map: LommesAddition of Kushite heartland पाटलिपुत्र (talk) Source: National Geographic 2019, CC BY-SA 4.0 <https://creativecommons.org/licenses/by-sa/4.0>, via Wikimedia Commons, https://commons.wikimedia.org/wiki/File:Kushite_heartland_and_Kushite_Empire_o f_the_25th_dynasty_circa_700_BCE.jpg

35 https://commons.wikimedia.org/wiki/File:Taharqa,_Louvre_Museum.jpg

36 Photograph by Rama, Wikimedia Commons, Cc-by-sa-2.0-fr, CC BY-SA 2.0 FR <https://creativecommons.org/licenses/by-sa/2.0/fr/deed.en>, via Wikimedia Commons, https://commons.wikimedia.org/wiki/File:Head_of_Nectanebo_II-MBA_Lyon_H1701-IMG_0204.jpg

37 https://commons.wikimedia.org/wiki/File:Philip_Galle_-_Lighthouse_of_Alexandria_(Pharos_of_Alexandria)_-_1572.jpg

38 https://commons.wikimedia.org/wiki/File:Cleopatra_and_Caesar_by_Jean-Leon-Gerome.jpg

39 https://commons.wikimedia.org/wiki/File:Jean-Baptiste_Regnault_-_Death_of_Cleopatra_-_Google_Art_Project.jpg

40 https://commons.wikimedia.org/wiki/File:Kleopatra-VII.-Altes-Museum-Berlin1.jpg

41 Jeff Dahl, CC BY-SA 4.0 <https://creativecommons.org/licenses/by-sa/4.0>, via Wikimedia Commons, https://commons.wikimedia.org/wiki/File:Eye_of_Horus_bw.svg

42 Amice M.Calverley, Alan Gardiner, 1935, CC BY-SA 4.0 <https://creativecommons.org/licenses/by-sa/4.0>, via Wikimedia Commons, https://commons.wikimedia.org/wiki/File:Sethos2-Disrobing-Amen-Re.jpg

43 https://commons.wikimedia.org/wiki/File:27.1_Iaru.tif

44 Jon Bodsworth, Copyrighted free use, via Wikimedia Commons, https://commons.wikimedia.org/wiki/File:Mastaba-faraoun-3.jpg

45 Nikola Smolenski, CC BY-SA 3.0 RS <https://creativecommons.org/licenses/by-sa/3.0/rs/deed.en>, via Wikimedia Commons, https://commons.wikimedia.org/wiki/File:Valley_of_the_Kings_panorama.jpg

46 Diego Delso, CC BY-SA 4.0 <https://creativecommons.org/licenses/by-sa/4.0>, via Wikimedia Commons, https://commons.wikimedia.org/wiki/File:Deir_el-Medina,_Luxor,_Egipto,_2022-04-03,_DD_18.jpg

www.ingramcontent.com/pod-product-compliance
Lightning Source LLC
Chambersburg PA
CBHW061745120626
46550CB00005B/1891